A Guided Tour of Computer Programming in BASIC

Thomas A. Dwyer

Michael S. Kaufman

Robert B. Davis, *Editorial Adviser*

HOUGHTON MIFFLIN COMPANY / BOSTON

ATLANTA   DALLAS   GENEVA, ILL.   HOPEWELL, N.J.   PALO ALTO

ABOUT THE AUTHORS

Thomas A. Dwyer is Associate Professor of Computer Science at the University of Pittsburgh, Pittsburgh, Pennsylvania. Dr. Dwyer has taught at the high school level as well as in college, and is currently Director of Project SOLO, an experiment in computing for secondary school systems.

Michael S. Kaufman is currently an undergraduate at Harvard University. He worked in Project SOLO at the University of Pittsburgh and at Pittsburgh's Taylor Allderdice High School.

EDITORIAL ADVISER

Robert B. Davis, currently on leave from Syracuse University, has assumed the positions of Director of the Curriculum Laboratory, Associate Director for Education of the Computer-Based Education Research Laboratory (PLATO Project), and Professor of Elementary Education, at the University of Illinois in Urbana-Champaign.

Illustrations by **Mark Kelley**

CREDITS
Page 3 Digital Equipment Corporation (left) Data General Corporation (right)
Page 5 Hewlett Packard
Page 6 Digital Equipment Corporation
Page 78 Teletype Corporation

Library of Congress Catalog Card Number: 72-4392

ISBN: 0-395-14716-6

Contents

1–1 Here's the Plan

1

Getting Ready for the Journey

Our tour of computer programming in BASIC is about to begin. Here's a quick idea of where we are headed, how we'll get there, and some of the more interesting things we'll meet along the way.

This book is divided into four parts:

PART 1 will tell you a little about computers and what to expect of them. It will also show you how to get the computer ready to "talk" to you (this is sometimes called *logging in*).

PARTS 2 AND 3 form the main part of the tour. They show you how to write computer programs. A *program* is a list of instructions that makes the computer work for you, following your wishes with great precision and speed.

PART 4 is where the fun begins. It introduces you to professional computer applications, including such things as an airline reservation system, automated game playing, and a program that "writes" payroll records.

As you go through the book, you'll find that you are frequently asked to stop reading, go to your computer, and try out the ideas you have just read about. Working directly with a machine in this way is called ON-LINE computing. The nice thing about ON-LINE computing is that it gives you an opportunity to experiment. Even if you make mistakes, the computer will just sit there, humming away, an obedient robot that doesn't know whether you are a beginning student or the world's greatest scientist.

You'll recognize ON-LINE sections by seeing ON-LINE printed in the margin as shown here. The reason actual computing is called "on-line" is that there is a direct connection between you and the computer made over a telephone *line,* or over similar wires. You'll see exactly how this is done in Sections 1–3 and 1–4.

Work which is done *without* a direct connection to a computer is called OFF-LINE. Examples of off-line work are reading the book, doing exercises which simulate (imitate) the action of a computer, drawing flow charts (explained on pages 47 and 54), and punching programs on paper tape (explained on pages 78–82). The best way to learn computer programming is to continually mix *off-line* preparation with *on-line* computing.

OFF-LINE

ON-LINE

When you are ON-LINE, you will be communicating with the computer in a "conversational" way, using a special language called BASIC. We'll have a lot to say about BASIC in this book, but let's first find out something about computers.

1–2 How to Recognize a Computer

The full name for the kind of computer we will study is "general purpose digital computer." From now on we'll simply refer to such machines as "computers," which is what everybody does anyway. The important thing for us now is learning how to use a computer.

Computers come in many sizes and shapes, but there are two general types you are likely to encounter.

The first of these is called a MINICOMPUTER system. As you can see from the name, the computing part of such a system is small in size — about as big as the average television set. Although there is some limit on the size of the problems that a "MINI" can handle, it is able to do very sophisticated things — including all the programs in this book.

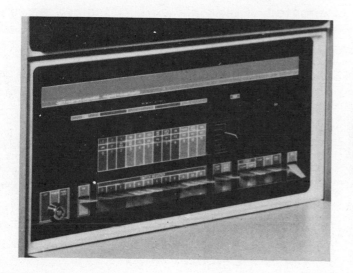 

Two Minicomputers

As the drawing at the left suggests, there are at least two parts to a minicomputer "system" (that's what "system" means — something with several parts). There is the box labeled MINI-COMPUTER and there is also an object called a TERMINAL. The terminal looks something like a typewriter. It is the means by which you and the computer will "talk" or *communicate* with each other.

The large arrows in the picture show that you communicate with the computer by typing instructions on the terminal keyboard, while the computer communicates back by printing information on the paper in the terminal.

A minicomputer is usually located right in the room with the person who is using it, and it is *usually* controlled with terminals. Why did we say "usually"? Because *some* minicomputers are controlled by dropping a deck of specially marked cards into a hopper on the machine. If you are using such a system, your teacher will show you how to mark such cards. You should also take a look at Section 4–5 in this book, which talks about "batch system" computers that use card input.

The second type of computer that you may use is the large machine that requires a room all to itself, and which may be many miles away. Such machines can also be controlled with terminals, but the terminals are hardly ever in the same room as the computer. This is no problem, since two-way communication with a computer can take place over telephone lines. The setup looks something like this:

Using this arrangement, many people can *simultaneously* communicate with a large, expensive computer. The process that makes this possible is called *time sharing*.

How does time sharing work? Because of the tremendous speed with which it carries out its operations, the computer can give each person all the computing time he needs in a fraction of each minute that he is connected to the computer. The *rest* of that minute can go to the other users (by "user" we mean anyone working at an on-line terminal). The situation is something like that of a grocery clerk taking telephone orders from several customers at the same time. If the clerk could switch back and forth from one telephone to another fast enough, each customer would think he was getting the clerk's full attention. The computer *is* that fast; you think it's talking only to you!

The picture at the top of page 5 shows the arrangement used by some time-sharing systems. The box labeled "multiplexor" is a

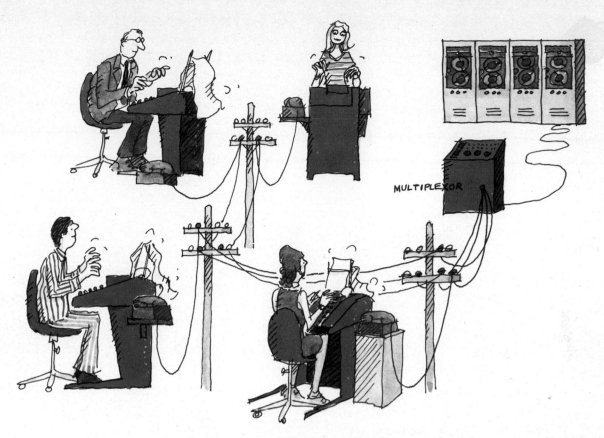

device that squeezes several computer conversations into one "leased" telephone line used exclusively for computing. Users need only dial a local number that connects them to the multiplexor.

A Large Time-Sharing Computer

To make things clearer, let's continue this discussion by considering the two types of computer systems separately. You need read only the section that corresponds to your type of computer (1–3 for minicomputers, 1–4 for time-sharing computers).

1-3 Getting Ready to Communicate with a MINICOMPUTER

There are three things you should do:

1. Make sure (by asking someone) that the MINICOMPUTER is turned on and ready to accept instructions written in BASIC. (It may be necessary to "load" something called the BASIC *compiler* into the computer. This will have to be done by someone familiar with your machine. That word "compiler" is explained on page 10.)

2. Check to see if the TERMINAL is switched on (if not, turn the knob to LINE).

Minicomputer with Terminal and Other Equipment

3. Type the letters SCR on the terminal (this is short for SCRatch; it erases anything that still might be left from the last person who used the computer) and then push the key marked RETURN (short for carriage return).

You're now ready to type in a program. Skip to Section 1-5.

1–4 Getting Ready to Communicate with a TIME-SHARING COMPUTER

You might want to glance enviously at the instructions for the mini-computer users. They had a rather simple explanation of how to get the computer ready. Time-sharing users will have more things to consider, although the process is much easier to do than to read about. The *exact* steps you should follow will depend on the particular time-sharing system that you are using, and the best way to learn is to have someone show you. The instructions that follow should help in a general way, however.

The first thing you have to do is call up your computer. Telephones are used with terminals in two ways. Check to see which type you have, and then read the correct column.

A. BUILT-IN TELEPHONE

1. Push the button marked ORIG.

2. Dial the telephone number of the computer. The computer should answer with a high-pitched whistle.
3. Probably, you should push the FDX button on the right side of the *terminal*. (There are some systems where you shouldn't push this button — ask to be sure.)
4. Now LOG IN as described below.

B. TELEPHONE SEPARATE FROM TERMINAL

1. Turn the knob on the terminal to LINE.
2. There should be a small box called an ACOUSTIC COUPLER near the telephone. Switch it ON.
3. Dial the telephone number of the computer. The computer should answer with a high-pitched whistle.
4. Place the telephone receiver into the coupler as shown in the diagram.

5. Now LOG IN as described below.

LOGGING IN is the process of identifying yourself to the computer. This is necessary because the computer has many people using it, and it has to know who you are in order to keep track of the work you do.

We'll show an example of logging in on one particular time-sharing system. After reading this, you should write down the procedure for the particular system you are using, since it may be a little different.

So that you can follow our discussion of logging in, we've included a picture of a terminal keyboard. It would be a good idea for you to locate the various keys as you read the rest of this part of the book. You will notice that the letters always print as capitals. You use the SHIFT key only when you want to type one of the symbols at the top of a key. For example, if you press (" / 2) the 2 will print. If you hold down the SHIFT key while pressing the same key, the " will print.

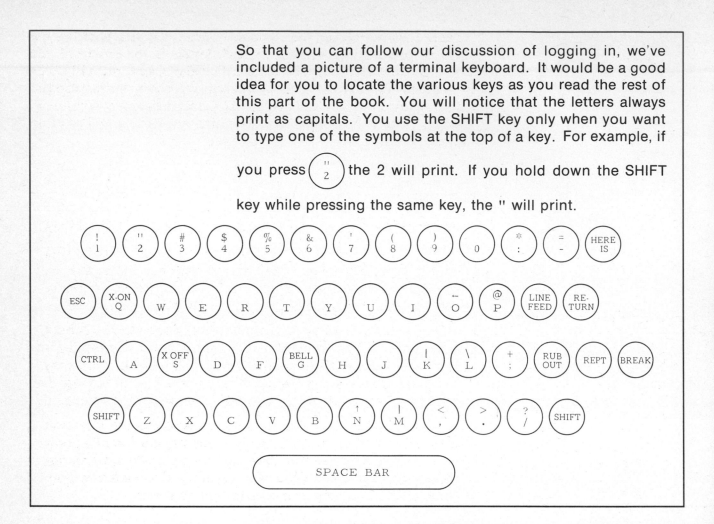

The method of **LOGGING IN** that we'll show you is that of Time Share Corporation in Hanover, New Hampshire 03755, which offers a time-sharing service. Since this service uses only the BASIC language, the LOG-IN is especially easy. You simply type in HELLO- followed by your identification number, a comma, and your password, as shown in the first line below. Notice that no spaces are typed in this line. Now press the carriage RETURN key. If you have done all this correctly, the computer will respond by typing a reply like the next two lines shown. On some Time Share Corporation connections, another line giving the time is included.

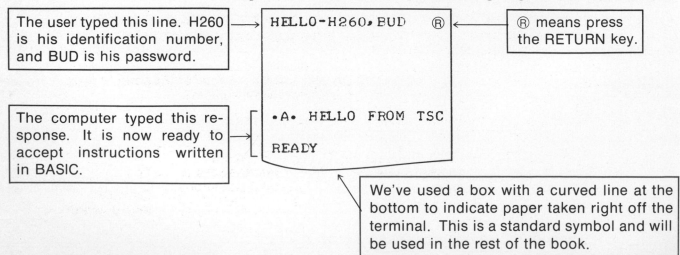

The user typed this line. H260 is his identification number, and BUD is his password.

HELLO-H260,BUD   ℝ

ℝ means press the RETURN key.

The computer typed this response. It is now ready to accept instructions written in BASIC.

•A• HELLO FROM TSC

READY

We've used a box with a curved line at the bottom to indicate paper taken right off the terminal. This is a standard symbol and will be used in the rest of the book.

Since anyone can see the password once it's typed, your teacher may tell you to insert secret "control" letters in the password you use. For example, you may be told that the password is BUP^{C}D. P^C is called "control P." You type it by *first* pressing the key marked CTRL, and then (while still holding the CTRL key down) pressing P. The computer will "know" you did this, but nothing will *print* on the page for unauthorized persons to see.

NOTES FOR USERS OF OTHER TIME-SHARING SYSTEMS

NOTE 1: In our example of logging in, the user was the first one to type. On some time-sharing systems, the computer types a short message (like the date) as soon as you connect the telephone. Then it's your turn.

NOTE 2: In our example, the computer was ready to accept programs written in BASIC right after log-in. On systems that offer other languages in addition to BASIC, you may have to type the word BASIC during some part of the log-in procedure to tell it which language you are going to use.

NOTE 3: Some time-sharing systems ask you the question NEW OR OLD? right after log-in. This means that the computer wants to know whether you are going to work on an old program that is stored in its memory or write a new one. Your teacher will tell you how to handle this.

FINAL CHECKLIST FOR TIME-SHARING USERS

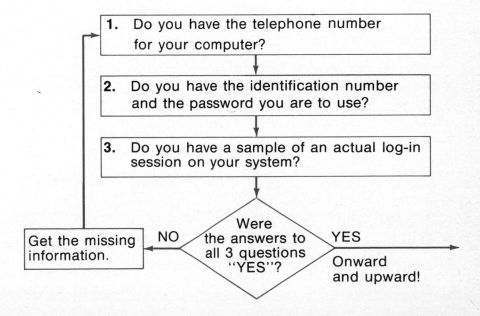

1. Do you have the telephone number for your computer?

2. Do you have the identification number and the password you are to use?

3. Do you have a sample of an actual log-in session on your system?

Were the answers to all 3 questions "YES"?

NO → Get the missing information.

YES → Onward and upward!

1–5 The BASIC Language

Now that you have the computer's attention, what do you say to it? Well, as you may suspect by now, the "conversation" that you carry on with a computer through a terminal can't be in ordinary English (or any other "natural" language). Instructions to a computer have to be written in a special *programming* language.

A number of such programming languages have been developed for "conversational" computing. The most popular of these, and by far the best one for any beginner to master, is called BASIC (*B*eginner's *A*ll-purpose *S*ymbolic *I*nstruction *C*ode).

Computers don't actually "understand" BASIC. They translate BASIC into machine code, something that looks very mysterious to human beings. The translation is done by a special program called the BASIC COMPILER. Fortunately, you don't have to know anything about the COMPILER, since it is used automatically anytime you RUN a BASIC program.

Sentences written in BASIC are called *statements*. Let's compare some BASIC statements with English sentences that we might use to instruct a robot-like character called XENON. We'll imagine that the English instructions are coming from a tape recorder. (Don't take this comparison too seriously; it's only meant to give you a rough idea of how the computer interprets BASIC.)

ENGLISH SENTENCES	BASIC STATEMENTS
Attention Xenon. This is H260,BUD speaking. Please memorize the following instructions. *Do not execute them until you are told to.*	HELLO-H260,BUD
1. The chalkboard behind your desk has several squares drawn on it. Write the letter X *next* to one of these, and then write the number 9 *inside* this square.	1 LET X=9
2. Now write the letter Y next to another square, and then write the number 12 inside the square.	2 LET Y=12

3. You'll find a large piece of paper on your desk. On the first line you are to print "PROBLEM 1."	3 PRINT "PROBLEM 1"
4. On the next line of this paper you are to print the *sum* of the number written next to X and the number written next to Y.	4 PRINT X+Y
5. On the next line of the paper you are to print "PROBLEM 2."	5 PRINT "PROBLEM 2"
6. On the next line of the paper you are to print the *product* of the number written next to X and the number written next to Y.	6 PRINT X∗Y (Notice that multiplication is indicated by ∗ in BASIC.)
7. This is the end of your instructions. ....STAND BY....	7 END
You are now commanded to execute the preceding instructions — Begin	RUN

By now you have undoubtedly noticed that BASIC uses very few words compared with English. BASIC also requires that you give your instructions in very small "steps" — one thing at a time.

We won't say any more about BASIC for now, since that's what the rest of this book is all about. If you didn't follow all of the preceding discussion, don't worry about it. We'll go through everything step-by-step in Part 2.

The important thing to do now is to get ON-LINE so that you can get a feel for how all of these ideas work on a real computer.

1-6 Putting It All Together

Here's a summary of how the things discussed so far go together during an ON-LINE session. There are really four major steps in any ON-LINE session.

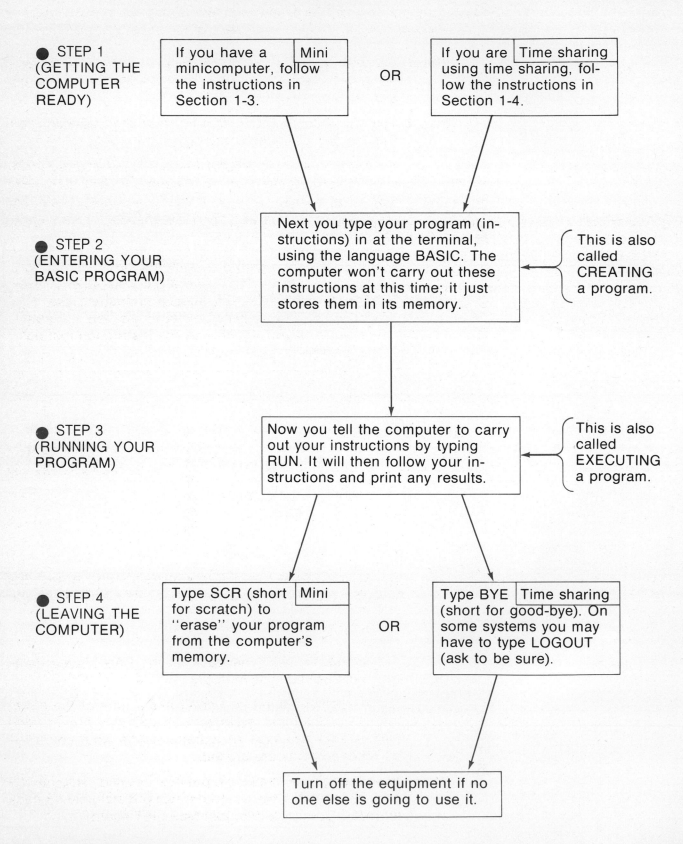

● STEP 1
(GETTING THE
COMPUTER
READY)

If you have a	Mini
minicomputer, follow the instructions in Section 1-3.	

OR

If you are	Time sharing
using time sharing, follow the instructions in Section 1-4.	

● STEP 2
(ENTERING YOUR
BASIC PROGRAM)

Next you type your program (instructions) in at the terminal, using the language BASIC. The computer won't carry out these instructions at this time; it just stores them in its memory.

This is also called CREATING a program.

● STEP 3
(RUNNING YOUR
PROGRAM)

Now you tell the computer to carry out your instructions by typing RUN. It will then follow your instructions and print any results.

This is also called EXECUTING a program.

● STEP 4
(LEAVING THE
COMPUTER)

Type SCR (short	Mini
for scratch) to "erase" your program from the computer's memory.	

OR

Type BYE	Time sharing
(short for good-bye). On some systems you may have to type LOGOUT (ask to be sure).	

Turn off the equipment if no one else is going to use it.

1-7 You're On!

The time has come for you to try out these ideas at a real computer terminal, even though you have not yet learned to write your own programs in BASIC. Follow the directions below. You can't hurt anything; so don't be afraid to make mistakes. (The examples in Sections 1–8 and 1–9 illustrate some of the things that may happen.)

Step 1 Get the computer ready by following the directions in Section 1–3 if you have a mini or Section 1–4 if you use time sharing.

Step 2 Type in your BASIC program. Use the example from Section 1–5 (remember Xenon?).

If you are in the middle of a line and make a typing error, press the RETURN key. The computer will then print ??? or a message saying it found an error. Press the RETURN key again and type the *entire* line over again.

> NOTE: Some computer systems have additional features for correcting errors, such as use of the ESCape key, or certain special characters like ←. You'll have to find out what these are on your system from your teacher or the instruction manual that came with your system.

Here's what you type:

```
1 LET X=9              ®
2 LET Y=12             ®
3 PRINT "PROBLEM1"     ®
4 PRINT X+Y            ®
5 PRINT "PROBLEM 2"    ®
6 PRINT X*Y            ®
7 END                  ®
```

® means press the RETURN key.

In case you have made a few mistakes and would like to be sure that you have corrected everything, just type:

```
LIST   ®
```

The computer will type back all the BASIC statements that it has stored in its memory.

If you see something you don't like in one of the statements (for example, statement 3), just type it over. The *last* version you type of statement 3 is what counts — all other versions are erased.

Even though you may have put in a "revised" statement 3 *after* statement 7, the computer will put statement 3 back in order. To check this, just type LIST again.

Step 3 Now you're ready to see the computer *execute* (carry out) your instructions. Simply type:

RUN ®

You can type RUN as often as you like. If you get tired of seeing the same answers, you can change some of the statements in your program. For example, you might type:

```
1 LET X=99 ®
2 LET Y=49 ®
RUN        ®
```

This changes statements 1 and 2 only; statements 3, 4, 5, 6, and 7 are still in the computer.

What do you think will happen?

> NOTE: If you wish to *delete* (get rid of) some statements, just type the line numbers followed by a carriage RETURN.
>
> EXAMPLE: If you type
>
> 3 ®
> 4 ®
>
> statements 3 and 4 will be erased from your program (forever).

Step 4 Leave the computer. If you are the last to use it for the time being, follow Step 4 of Section 1–6.

1–8 Example of a Perfect Session

Let's first show what happens when someone follows the preceding directions without making a single mistake (which just about *never* happens!).

> NOTE: The rest of the examples in this book are shown as run on a terminal connected to the computer of Time Share Corporation, Hanover, New Hampshire 03755.
>
> The details of logging in and out, the wording of error messages (shown in the next section), and the manner of correcting typing errors may differ slightly on other systems. However, all the BASIC programs in this book will run on other systems.

Here's our perfect session (notice that this student has made statements 3 and 5 a little "fancier"). From now on we won't show pressing the RETURN key; this must be done after every line typed by the user.

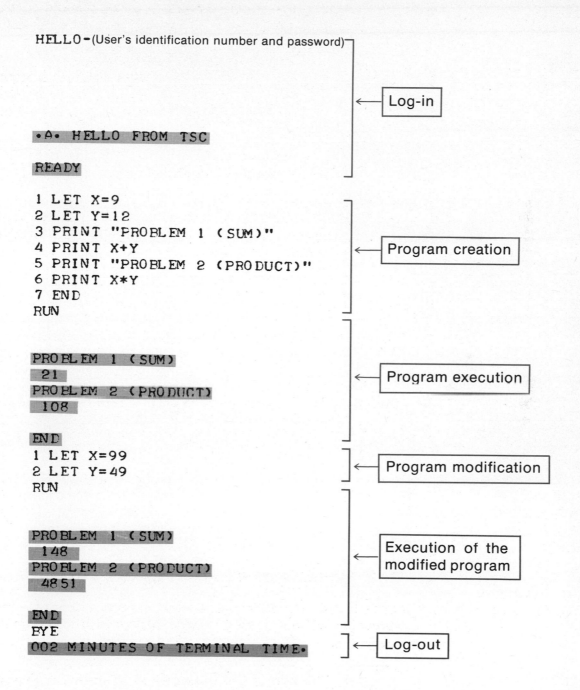

```
HELLO -(User's identification number and password)
```
← Log-in

```
•A• HELLO FROM TSC

READY
```

```
1 LET X=9
2 LET Y=12
3 PRINT "PROBLEM 1 (SUM)"
4 PRINT X+Y
5 PRINT "PROBLEM 2 (PRODUCT)"
6 PRINT X*Y
7 END
RUN
```
← Program creation

```
PROBLEM 1 (SUM)
 21
PROBLEM 2 (PRODUCT)
 108
```
← Program execution

```
END
1 LET X=99
2 LET Y=49
RUN
```
← Program modification

```
PROBLEM 1 (SUM)
 148
PROBLEM 2 (PRODUCT)
 4851
```
← Execution of the modified program

```
END
BYE
002 MINUTES OF TERMINAL TIME•
```
← Log-out

HELLO–(User's identification number and password)

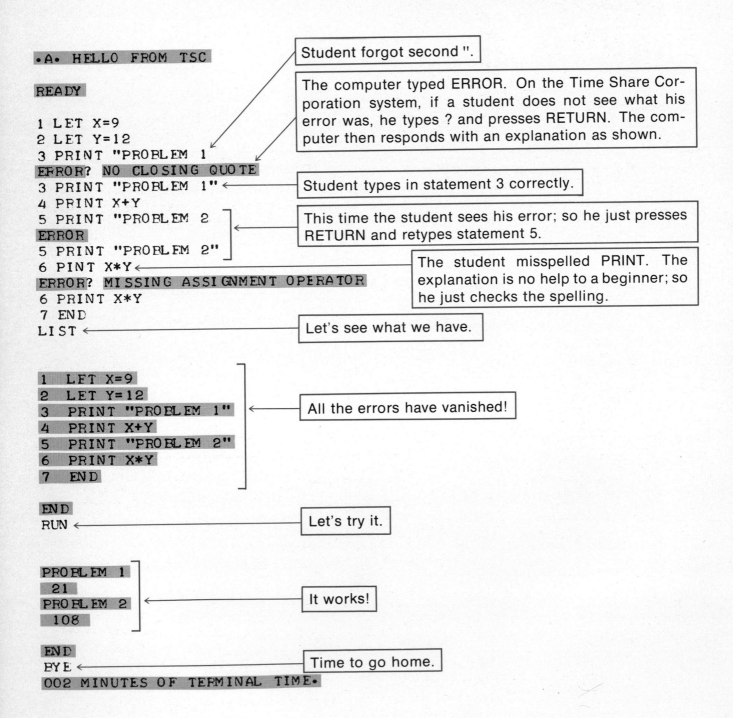

```
.A. HELLO FROM TSC
```
Student forgot second ".

```
READY
```
The computer typed ERROR. On the Time Share Corporation system, if a student does not see what his error was, he types ? and presses RETURN. The computer then responds with an explanation as shown.

```
1 LET X=9
2 LET Y=12
3 PRINT "PROBLEM 1
ERROR? NO CLOSING QUOTE
3 PRINT "PROBLEM 1"
```
Student types in statement 3 correctly.

```
4 PRINT X+Y
5 PRINT "PROBLEM 2
ERROR
5 PRINT "PROBLEM 2"
```
This time the student sees his error; so he just presses RETURN and retypes statement 5.

```
6 PINT X*Y
ERROR? MISSING ASSIGNMENT OPERATOR
6 PRINT X*Y
```
The student misspelled PRINT. The explanation is no help to a beginner; so he just checks the spelling.

```
7 END
LIST
```
Let's see what we have.

```
1   LET X=9
2   LET Y=12
3   PRINT "PROBLEM 1"
4   PRINT X+Y
5   PRINT "PROBLEM 2"
6   PRINT X*Y
7   END
```
All the errors have vanished!

```
END
RUN
```
Let's try it.

```
PROBLEM 1
 21
PROBLEM 2
 108
```
It works!

```
END
BYE
002 MINUTES OF TERMINAL TIME.
```
Time to go home.

One last suggestion — it will be a good idea to save your first successful program as a guide for your next ON-LINE session.

1–10 More Programs for You to Try

The rest of this book will be devoted to the "art of programming" in the BASIC language. However, you may want to run another program or two just for the fun of it before reading on. Here are two short programs you can try. We won't explain them here at all, and we won't tell you what happens when they execute. You'll find out after you type RUN.

Program 1
```
10  PRINT "THIS IS A COMPUTER"
20  FOR K=1 TO 4
30  PRINT "NOTHING CAN GO"
40  FOR J=1 TO 3
50  PRINT "WRONG"
60  NEXT J
70  NEXT K
80  FND
RUN
```

Program 2
```
10  LET Y=1970
20  LET P=200
30  PRINT "YEAR", "MILLIONS OF PEOPLE"
40  PRINT Y,P
50  LET Y=Y+5
60  LET P=1.2*P
70  IF Y>2070 THEN 90
80  GOTO 40
90  END
RUN
```

Remember — you're not expected to understand how these programs work (you will at the end of Part 2 of this book). They are given here in case you want to try out your computer system and become more familiar with using a terminal. You'll also find that the experience will help you understand things a great deal better when you return to reading.

2–1 The Basic Vocabulary of BASIC

Now that you know how to manage an ON-LINE session with your favorite computer, we can turn our attention to showing you how to write your own programs in BASIC. We'll do this in Part 2 by concentrating on a dozen *key words* in the BASIC language. The amazing thing is that you will get along very well with this small vocabulary and be able to write interesting programs for the computer. (In case you're wondering, Part 3 of the book will extend your vocabulary to include about as many more key words.)

Each section in Part 2 will show you how to use a few key words to make BASIC *statements.* And once you have learned how to put a couple of statements together, you'll have a program. It's as simple as that — key words are used to make statements, and statements are used to make programs.

The *key words* that we'll study in Part 2 of this book are:

    PRINT
    END
    LET
    INPUT
    GOTO
    IF . . . THEN
    STOP
    FOR . . . (STEP)
    NEXT

In addition to these key words, we'll also use the three *commands* that you have already met:

    LIST
    RUN
    SCR   (SCR is short for SCRATCH)

2

The Economy Tour

What's the difference between a key word and a command? A key word is never used *alone*. It's always *part* of a BASIC statement that has some other parts to it. (We'll soon learn what these other parts are.) Commands, on the other hand, are used by themselves.

For example, here's a silly little BASIC program with two statements followed by a command:

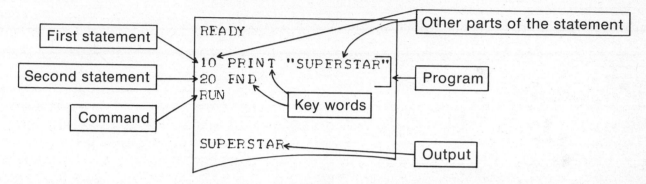

Statements are instructions to the computer. The computer stores these instructions in its "memory," but it doesn't *execute* them (carry them out) until you say so. You do this by typing the command RUN. Then the computer executes all of your instructions. Any results that it prints out after you tell it to RUN are called OUTPUT.

> NOTE: The word READY at the top of the program shown above is printed by most computers after you have logged in correctly. It means that the computer is *ready* to accept a BASIC program.
>
> Most computers also print a message *after* you run a program to indicate that the OUTPUT is complete (END, DONE, RAN, and so on). The Time Share Corporation system types END (not shown in the print-out above).

2–2 BASIC Statements Using the Key Words PRINT and END

Let's look at the outline of a BASIC program that uses only two key words: PRINT and END.

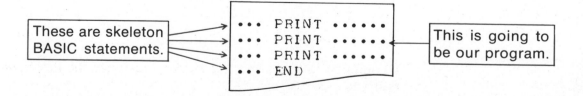

The dots mean that something is missing and must be inserted in these positions before we have real BASIC statements.

To illustrate what the missing parts of a PRINT statement may be, let's look at an example of a program with three PRINT statements and one END statement:

```
READY

10    PRINT "DEMONSTRATION"
20    PRINT "2+2 IS"
30    PRINT 2+2
40    END
RUN


DEMONSTRATION
2+2 IS
 4
```

The first thing you should notice is that every BASIC statement starts with a *line number*. This can be any whole number from 1 to 9999 (do *not* use commas in writing large numbers for a computer). The line numbers serve as a guide to the computer in RUNning the program, telling it in what *order* it should carry out your instructions.

Next comes a key word. Suppose that the key word is PRINT. What comes next?

One kind of thing that can follow PRINT is shown in statement 10 in our example:

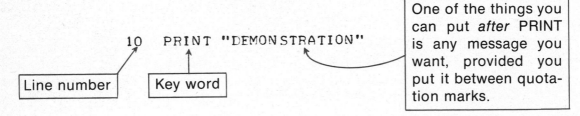

One of the things you can put *after* PRINT is any message you want, provided you put it between quotation marks.

When you say RUN, the computer will obediently print back whatever was typed between the quotation marks; however there is *one* thing you can't have inside the quotation marks — you can't have another quotation mark. If you say, for example,

10 PRINT "THAT'S A "HOT" ISSUE"

to a computer, it will not print what you want. It may not accept the statement at all and simply print ERROR.

To get around this limitation, you can use single quotation marks as shown at the right.

```
READY

10 PRINT "THAT'S A 'HOT' ISSUE"
20 END
RUN


THAT'S A 'HOT' ISSUE
```

What else can we put after **PRINT**? Take a look at line 30 of our example. In this statement we *didn't* use quotes:

    30 PRINT 2+2

When we **RUN** the program, the computer will print 4 for line 30. In other words, if you don't use quotation marks, the computer will *calculate* what's there, and then print the answer.

> MORAL: If you don't use quotation marks, you had better have a number or a numerical expression that can be calculated using arithmetic. (Later on you'll learn to use variables.)

By now you have probably noticed the symbols that computers use for doing arithmetic:

> \+ means add
> \- means subtract
> * means multiply (don't use ×)
> / means divide (you're not allowed to use ÷)

These symbols are also called operators. There is one other operator used by computers:

> ↑ means exponentiate

(Some computers use ** instead of ↑.) Don't let that word "exponentiate" worry you. All it means is repeated multiplication. Thus,

3↑4 is shorthand for 3∗3∗3∗3. In other words, 3↑4 means "take the product of *four* threes." Watch:

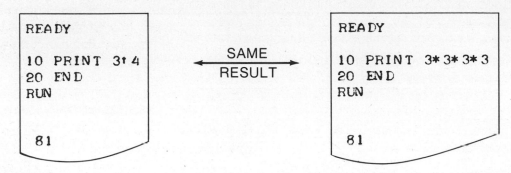

```
READY

10  PRINT  3↑4
20  END
RUN


    81
```

← SAME RESULT →

```
READY

10  PRINT  3∗3∗3∗3
20  END
RUN


    81
```

```
READY

10   PRINT  8+4
20   PRINT  8-4
30   PRINT  8∗4
40   PRINT  8/4
50   PRINT  8•0/4•0
60   PRINT  •5∗8
70   PRINT  3↑3
80   PRINT  10•8-7•7
90   PRINT  3+4-6
100  PRINT  5∗4+3
110  PRINT  4+3∗5
120  END
```

19
23
1
3•1
27
4
2
2
32
4
12

RUN

Exercise 1 Write down the *output* you think a computer would produce after it got the signal to RUN the program shown at the left. (This is called *simulating* a computer run. It's very good practice and it can come in very handy when you are trying to find a "bug" (error) in a program.)

Check your answers with those printed upside down at the left.

Don't feel bad if you were puzzled by statements 100 and 110. There is really no way to predict what

　　　　100 PRINT 5∗4+3　　　or　　　110 PRINT 4+3∗5

will do unless you know that computer scientists once agreed that multiplication should be done before addition in a given problem. Thus, in line 110 the computer will *first* calculate that 3∗5 is 15, and *then* add 4 to get the answer 19.

But suppose that's not what you want — then you must use parentheses. If you type

　　　　110 PRINT (4+3)∗5

then the computer must first calculate what's inside the parentheses. This means it *first* finds that 4+3 is 7, and then it multiplies this 7 by 5 to get the answer 35.

PRACTICAL RULE: When asking the computer to PRINT answers to arithmetic problems, group things together the way you want them with parentheses. Be sure that every left parenthesis has a matching right parenthesis.

FORMAL RULES:
(1) If there are no parentheses, the computer performs operations by going from left to right *three* times. The first time, all exponentiation operations (↑ or **) are done. The second time, * and / operations are done in order from left to right. The third time, + and − are done in order from left to right.

EXAMPLE: 3+5*2↑3−4/2*3   becomes 3+5*8−4/2*3
                            then 3+40−6
                            then 37

(2) If there are parentheses, the computer looks for the first *right* parenthesis, backs up to the matching left parenthesis, and then applies rule (1) to convert everything inside this *inner* pair of parentheses to a single number. These parentheses are then thrown away, and the process is repeated. If you use several pairs of parentheses, the computer works from the "inside" out.

EXAMPLE: ((3+5)*3)/4   becomes (8*3)/4
                           then 6

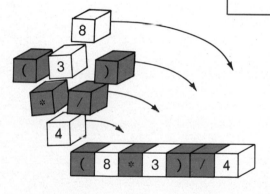

When in doubt, use parentheses. They can't do any harm — and they may make the difference between a right or a wrong answer.

Exercise 2 Copy and complete the following:
(a) 4+9=___?___
(b) (4+9)=___?___
(c) (4+9)*2=___?___
(d) 4+(9*2)=___?___
(e) (4+(9*2))*3=___?___
(f) (4+(9*2))*(3+1)=___?___
(g) .5*((8+(9*2))*(3+1))=___?___
  ↑

NOTE: .5 is the same as 0.5 to the computer.

Here are several different computer programs using PRINT. Simulate running each of these by writing down the output you would produce if you were a computer.

Exercise 3 Simulate running this program.

```
10   PRINT 42+44
20   PRINT "AND"
30   PRINT 3*33
40   PRINT "ARE TWO SECRET AGENTS."
50   END
```

Exercise 4   Simulate running this program.

```
10    PRINT "WHAT HAPPENED IN THE YEAR"
20    PRINT 1000+776
30    PRINT "OR"
40    PRINT (5*200)+(2*450)+(9*5)
50    PRINT "OR"
60    PRINT ((5*(5*16)/4)*5*(2↑2))+1
70    END
```

Let's see what else we can do with the PRINT statement. For one thing, we can do several problems on one line.

EXAMPLE:

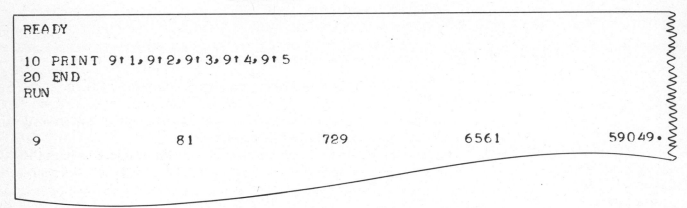

```
READY

10 PRINT 9↑1,9↑2,9↑3,9↑4,9↑5
20 END
RUN


9              81            729            6561           59049.
```

The computer calculated the answers to five problems for us and printed them *on the same line*. Notice what the comma does. When commas are used in a PRINT statement, they space the answers into 5 parts called *zones:*

Zone 1	Zone 2	Zone 3	Zone 4	Zone 5
9	81	729	6561	59049.
←—15 spaces—→	←—15 spaces—→	←—15 spaces—→	←—15 spaces—→	←—12 spaces—→
ΛΛΛΛΛΛΛΛΛΛΛΛΛΛΛ	ΛΛΛΛΛΛΛΛΛΛΛΛΛΛΛ	ΛΛΛΛΛΛΛΛΛΛΛΛΛΛΛ	ΛΛΛΛΛΛΛΛΛΛΛΛΛΛΛ	ΛΛΛΛΛΛΛΛΛΛΛΛ

If there are more than five items in the PRINT statement, the computer will go to the next line:

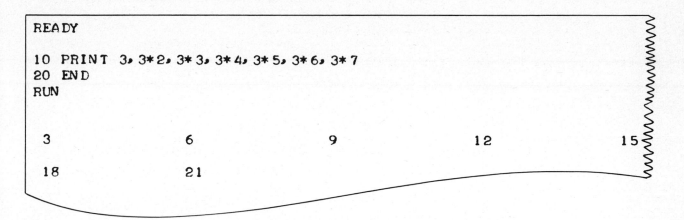

```
READY

10 PRINT 3, 3*2, 3*3, 3*4, 3*5, 3*6, 3*7
20 END
RUN


3            6            9           12          15

18          21
```

Another mark of punctuation you should know about is the semicolon. What the semicolon does varies somewhat from computer to computer, but it is always true that the semicolon leaves less space between answers than the comma.

On the Time Share Corporation system, the semicolon puts the answers as close together as possible. There will be one space between positive numbers because space is left for a possible negative sign.

To see the difference between what a comma does and what a semicolon does on this system, look at the following example. (Your computer may do things slightly differently.)

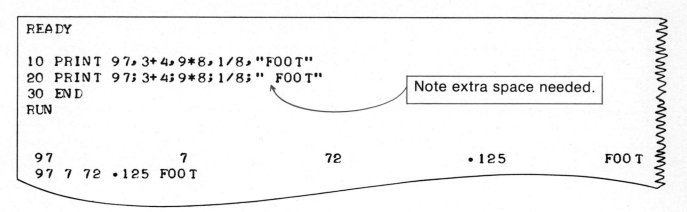

```
READY

10 PRINT 97, 3+4, 9*8, 1/8, "FOOT"
20 PRINT 97; 3+4; 9*8; 1/8; " FOOT"     [Note extra space needed.]
30 END
RUN


97           7           72          .125         FOOT
97 7 72 .125 FOOT
```

QUICK SUMMARY: If you want output spread out, use a comma; if you want output put close together, use a semicolon. Of course, the comma and semicolon are only used when you want more than one item on the same line.

Let's take time out to try some of these ideas on a computer. Before going ON-LINE, you probably should review the section on correcting typing errors (page 16).

(From now on we'll give our ON-LINE programs code names for easy reference.)

ON-LINE

Code Name: /ARITH/

Run the following program on your computer.

```
READY

10    PRINT "147 + 38 =";147+38
20    PRINT 5280*5;" FEET IN 5 MILES"
30    PRINT "THERE ARE";26*26*26;" THREE-LETTER CODE NAMES."
40    PRINT "COMPARISON OF 22/7 AND 355/113:";22/7,355/113
50    END
RUN
```

After you get this program to work, go on to /ARITH2/.

ON-LINE   ON-LINE   ON-LINE   ON-LINE

WARNING   WARNING   WARNING   WARNING

Before you do the next ON-LINE program, notice that its line numbers start with 100. If you had typed it in right after /ARITH/, the computer would have tried to put the two programs together with statements 10 to 50 followed by statements 100 to 150.

Do you see that if you were then to type RUN, the computer would ignore lines 100 to 150? It wouldn't look past the END statement in line 50. So, even though you were trying to RUN /ARITH2/, all you would get would be /ARITH/ once again.

To avoid this difficulty, you must get rid of the old program before typing in the new one. You do this by typing SCR and pressing RETURN. To check that there is no program there, type LIST. The computer will let you know in some way that there is no program there. On Time Share Corporation installations, the typing would look like this:

```
SCR
LIST  ⟵       There was nothing to LIST
END
```

MORAL: SCRatch the old before bringing in the new. Check with a LISTing.

RUN the following program; experiment with changes in it.

```
READY

100    PRINT "HAT SIZES IN DECIMAL FORM"
110    PRINT 6+5/8; 6+3/4; 6+7/8; 7; 7+1/8; 7+1/4; 7+3/8
120    PRINT "DRILL SIZES"
130    PRINT 1/32, 2/32, 3/32, 4/32, 5/32, 6/32, 7/32, 8/32
140    PRINT "MONEY AFTER DOUBLING $1 FOR 15 DAYS = $"; 2↑15
150    END
RUN
```

MAY 1   MAY 2   MAY 3....   MAY 15

By now you are probably discouraged by the amount of typing you have to do to get a little output. The trouble is that you can't write very interesting programs if the only key words you know are PRINT and END. So we'll sneak in two extra key words (FOR and NEXT, which we'll discuss in detail later) to help make this on-line session more interesting. *You aren't expected to understand what these key words do at this time.* Just type them in as shown.

NOTE: Code names with double slashes indicate extra on-line programs.

```
READY

10    PRINT " MULTIPLICATION TABLES FOR 10, 11, AND 12"
20    PRINT " ----------------------------------------"
30    PRINT
40    FOR X=1 TO 12
50    PRINT X; "*10="; X*10, X; "*11="; X*11, X; "*12="; X*12
60    NEXT X
70    END
RUN
```

NOTE: PRINT with nothing after it produces what is called a *line feed*. This means that the paper "feeds" up one extra line. Thus, the effect of line 30 above is to put a blank line in the OUTPUT, making it look neater.

LET'S REVIEW SECTION 2-2

● Different forms of the PRINT statement look like the following:

```
123 PRINT 45
50  PRINT 900/450
36  PRINT "HELLO THERE"
900 PRINT 10, 10*2, 10*3, 5↑7*3, ((16+32)/8)*123
20  PRINT 3+1; "SCORE AND"; 4+3; "YEARS AGO"
```

If more than one expression is used (as in lines 900 and 20 above), the following punctuation marks are used to separate the output:

(,) A comma separates the output up to 15 spaces:

```
10 PRINT "2","3","4"    gives

2              3              4
```

```
10 PRINT 2,3,4   gives (note space for sign)

 2              3              4
```

(;) A semicolon prints the outputs close together:

```
10 PRINT "2";"3";"4"    gives

234
```

```
10 PRINT 2;3;4    gives

 2  3  4
```

● An END statement is always needed as the last line of a program. It consists simply of a line number and END.

● RUN is the command which tells the computer to execute all the statements in its memory. Since RUN is *not* a statement, it never has a line number.

● SCR means scratch. It is a command which *erases* the previous program from the computer's memory. It never has a line number.

● LIST is a command that causes the computer to type out all the statements it has in its memory at the present time. It never has a line number.

2–3 Statements Using the Key Word [LET]

It's election time, and the votes for the three leading candidates have just been tallied. Flamboyant has 8497 votes, Handsome has 7231 votes, and Moderate topped the group with 9821 votes. Here's how the workers at election headquarters have "stored" this information on the chalkboard in the back room.

Our picture shows three spaces or *locations* on the board, called F, H, and M. We can think of F, H, and M as *labels* pasted on the board. Next to each of these labels is written the number of votes "stored" in our chalkboard memory. These numbers can, of course, be erased at any time, and new numbers can be put in each location.

Now let's use this picture to get a feel for what goes on in computer memories. We can also "store" numbers in the memory of a computer. In order to know where these numbers are being kept, we must also use *labels* for the various memory locations.

The LET statement in BASIC does both of these things at once.

● It gives a label to the memory location.

● It stores a number in this memory location.

For example, the statement

    20 LET F=8497

● Gives the label F to a location in the computer memory.

● Stores the number 8497 in the memory location having that label. The number 8497 is called the *contents* of the memory location F.

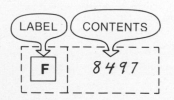

29

Labels are sometimes compared to the names on mailboxes as shown in the picture on the right. Notice that the *label* is very different from the *contents* of the box.

One mailbox has the *label* Smith, but it *contains* a letter.

We might call the label Smith a *variable* because the material put into the "Smith" mailbox can *vary*: one day a letter, the next day a magazine.

In a similar way, the labels used for memory locations in a computer are called *variables*. This is because different numbers can be stored in a computer memory location; its contents can *vary*. In BASIC, the names we use for labels are usually single letters such as A, B, C, X, Y.

The actual memories of computers don't look like chalkboards or mailboxes, of course. However, a person who wants to program a computer doesn't have to know about the actual construction of memories, and for our purposes the chalkboard picture is better.

F	~~230~~ ~~565~~ 8497 _ _ _ _ _ _
H	~~114~~ ~~429~~ 7231 _ _ _ _ _ _
M	~~375~~ ~~745~~ 9821 _ _ _ _ _ _

For one thing, we see that we can *erase* the number next to a label and put in a new number. This is exactly what computers do in their electronic memories. If we put a new number in the same location as an old number, the first number is erased.

If a BASIC program says

    10 LET A=4

we may imagine that the computer's memory looks like this:

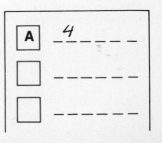

If we now say

      20 LET A=12

here is what the memory looks like:

The 4 is gone (forever), and a 12 is now in its place.

A	_12_ _ _ _
☐	_ _ _ _ _
☐	_ _ _ _ _

> In computer language, we say that memories have the property of *destructive read in*; that is, when we "read in" the 12, we destroy the 4.

```
READY

5 LET A=5*5
10 PRINT "A =";A
15 LET A=6*6
20 PRINT "A =";A
25 END
RUN


A = 25
A = 36
```

One big difference between a computer and a chalkboard is that the computer can do arithmetic on the numbers on the right side of a LET statement *before* storing the answer in its memory (the chalkboard just stands there). In the statement

      5 LET A=5*5

the computer *first* calculates 5*5 and *then* stores the answer (25) in location A. The statement

      15 LET A=6*6

stores 36 in location A, wiping out the 25.

SUGGESTION: It will help if you read LET statements from right to left. In the statement

      5 LET A=5*5

the computer calculates what's on the right side (using special arithmetic circuits). It then stores the answer in memory location A. You can imagine that the process looks like this:

Let's apply all of this discussion by writing a program to give us the total votes in our election (the one with Flamboyant, Handsome, and Moderate). To make life interesting, we'll also have our program PRINT out the *percent* of votes that each candidate received. You may recall that such a percent is found as follows:

Percent of votes received by a candidate
= (number of votes received/total number of
votes)∗ 100

This formula is used in lines 60, 70, and 80 of the following program.

```
READY

10   LET F=8497
20   LET H=7231
30   LET M=9821
40   LET T=F+H+M
50   PRINT "TOTAL NO. OF VOTES CAST IS"; T
60   PRINT "% FOR FLAMBOYANT ="; (F/T)*100; "%"
70   PRINT "% FOR HANDSOME ="; (H/T)*100; "%"
80   PRINT "% FOR MODERATE ="; (M/T)*100; "%"
90   END
RUN


TOTAL NO. OF VOTES CAST IS 25549
% FOR FLAMBOYANT = 33.2577%
% FOR HANDSOME = 28.3025%
% FOR MODERATE = 38.4399%
```

Notice that 33.2577+28.3025+38.4399=100.0001 instead of exactly 100. This is because the computer *rounded off* its answers. Round-off error isn't serious in this example (what's .0001% among friends!), but it can sometimes cause trouble if the programmer lets it "pile up" too much.

SUMMARY OF THE THINGS THAT CAN BE USED IN A LET STATEMENT:

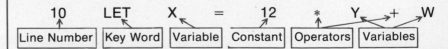

10	LET	X	=	12	∗ Y	+ W
Line Number	Key Word	Variable	Constant		Operators	Variables

X, Y, and W are called *variables,* since different numbers can be stored in the locations they represent. The number 12 is called a constant because it doesn't change.

In BASIC you're allowed to use only *one* variable on the left side of the equal sign (=) in a LET statement, and as many as you want on the right side. Constants can be used only on the right side.

Let's watch some LET statements in action. On the left we'll show a BASIC program. On the right we'll "picture" what happens inside the computer.

BASIC PROGRAM   MEMORY

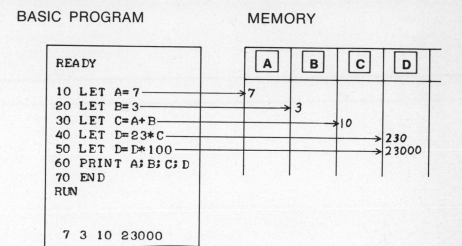

Did you catch what happened in statement 50? The computer worked on the *right* side of the statement first, calculating D*100, when the D location still had 230 in it from the previous step. *Then* it took the answer (23000) and put it back in location D. This means that the 230 was *erased*, and *replaced* by 23000.

Notice that the computer has an inexhaustible supply of constants. You name it, and you've got it!

So far we have used *single letters* for variable names. That gave us 26 names for VARIABLES.

NOTE: To avoid confusion between the letter O and the numeral zero, we will write zero as Ø when it is necessary to make a distinction.

In BASIC you can also use a single letter followed by a single digit for a variable name. Examples are:

A5, B7, D8, X9, Y1, Y2, Y3, AØ

This gives us 260 additional names for variables!

Exercise 1 Which of the following variable names are allowed in BASIC, and which are not allowed?

A   B   C8   C23   XY   2D   5F   W8   W13
W2   H7   O9   I1   J9   IOU   F-2   3   X3.1

Exercise 2 Simulate the RUN of the following program. Copy and fill in the chart at the right, showing the locations of memory, as you proceed.

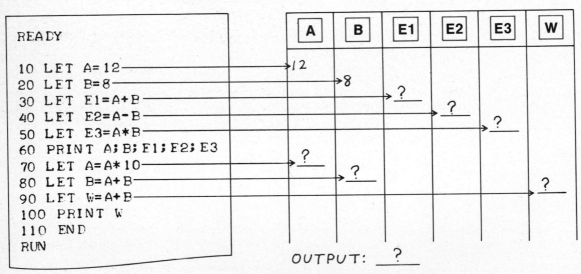

```
READY

10 LET A=12
20 LET B=8
30 LET E1=A+B
40 LET E2=A-B
50 LET E3=A*B
60 PRINT A; B; E1; E2; E3
70 LET A=A*10
80 LET B=A+B
90 LET W=A+B
100 PRINT W
110 END
RUN
```

A	B	E1	E2	E3	W
12	8	?	?	?	
?	?				?

OUTPUT: ___?___

Exercise 3 Simulate a RUN of the program shown at the right. Make a chart like that for Exercise 2, and fill in the memory locations as you proceed.

```
10 LET A=3*4
20 LET B=10*A
30 LET C=B/4+6
40 PRINT A; B; C
50 LET A=B+C
60 PRINT A
70 END
```

Exercise 4 (One last check to make sure you're ready for the next ON-LINE session.) Look at the "program" shown at the right. In each line there is an error. Find each error and re-write the lines in a form that makes sense. (It is impossible to guess what the original programmer had in mind; so there is no one "right" way to correct each line.)

```
10 LET A−2=4
20 PRIN 4
30 LET 4=C
40 PRINT,C,A
50 LET C/3=6
60 LET A=C+
70 PRINT AC
80 LET D=4 X A
90 PRINT THE ANSWER IS D
100 EMD
```

Code Name: /RAT1/

You are the program director of a national TV network, ABS (All-purpose Broadcasting System). And it's that time of year again; the Illson rating service reports are in, which means that you have to make your annual appearance before the Board of Directors with a list showing what percent of the audience ABS had for each of the "prime" hours (7 P.M. to 11 P.M.).

For each time slot, you must provide the total number of viewers, the number of viewers watching ABS, and then the percentage of viewers watching ABS. Your meeting with the Board is in just half an hour, and your list of percentages still isn't ready. Can the computer help? Let's find out. Here's a partial picture of the computer OUTPUT you'd like. The numbers of viewers came from the Illson survey.

TIME SLOT	TOTAL VIEWERS	VIEWERS OF ABS	% WATCHING ABS
1	31546	8876	
2	36530•	9604	
3	47867•	16390	
4	35483•	6379	

Write a program, using a series of LET and PRINT statements, which will output a complete chart. The formula you need for the last column in the chart is:

$$\text{Percent watching ABS} = \left(\frac{\text{No. of viewers of ABS}}{\text{Total No. of viewers}}\right) * 100$$

Your program should first PRINT headings. Then for the first time slot, here's what you might do:

```
LET N=1
LET A=the total number of viewers
LET B=the number of viewers watching ABS
LET C=(B/A)*100
```

Then PRINT N, A, B, C. Now repeat the process for N=2, and so on. Of course, you'll have to write statements in correct BASIC with line numbers, sticking exactly to the rules you've seen so far. When you've done this and are pretty sure your program is correct, take it to the computer and RUN it.

Code Name: //RATSTUDY//

In order to make this next program more interesting, we're going to sneak in the FOR and NEXT statements again *without explanation* (it's coming soon). We'll use them to write a program that shows how the % ratings of ABS in time slot 1 would change for *each extra* thousand viewers added until ABS had 30,876 people watching their shows.

The program is printed at the top of page 37.

RUN it and see if you can figure out how it works. (If you can't, wait until Section 2–7).

```
READY

10 PRINT "RATING STUDY FOR TIME SLOT 1"
20 PRINT "TOTAL VIEWERS","VIEWERS OF ABS"," % WATCHING ABS"
30 LET A=31546
40 LET B=8876
50 FOR X=1 TO 22
60 LET B=B+1000
70 PRINT A,B,(B/A)*100; "%"
80 NEXT X
90 END
RUN
```

LET'S REVIEW SECTION 2-3

● The LET statement is used to "assign a value to a variable." This means that the value (number) is stored in the computer's memory in a location which has a label, or "address," that is given by the variable's name. For example:

BASIC STATEMENT   PICTURE OF COMPUTER MEMORY

10 LET M=16+4

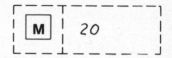

The value 20 is stored in the computer's memory in a location that has the address, or label, called M. The RIGHT side of the BASIC statement is calculated first, and then stored in the location named on the LEFT side.

● Variable names can be single letters (A, B, C, . . . , X, Y, Z) or single letters followed by single digits (such as A1, B7, W∅, X3).

2-4 The INPUT Statement

You probably found that your television-viewers program in Section 2-3 consisted of many repeated statements. For example, for each time slot, you had to have several LET statements. You may have had something like this:

    LET N=Time slot no.
    LET A=Total viewers
    LET B=Viewers of ABS
    LET C=(B/A)*100 (% watching ABS)
    PRINT N, A, B, C

. . . . which means that a set of similar statements had to be used for each time slot. Well, that's not very good programming.

Let's see if we can write a better program. We'll keep A, B, and C meaning the same things as listed on page 37. First, let's write the essential statements:

30 LET C=(B/A)*100 ←— That's a good start.
40 PRINT A,B,C;"%" ←— We have to PRINT the answers to get OUTPUT.
100 END

Of course, this program would not work because it has no values for A and B. To give A and B values, we'll use a new kind of BASIC statement — the INPUT statement.

Let's add two statements at the beginning of our program:

10 INPUT A
20 INPUT B

Here's what a few RUNs look like:

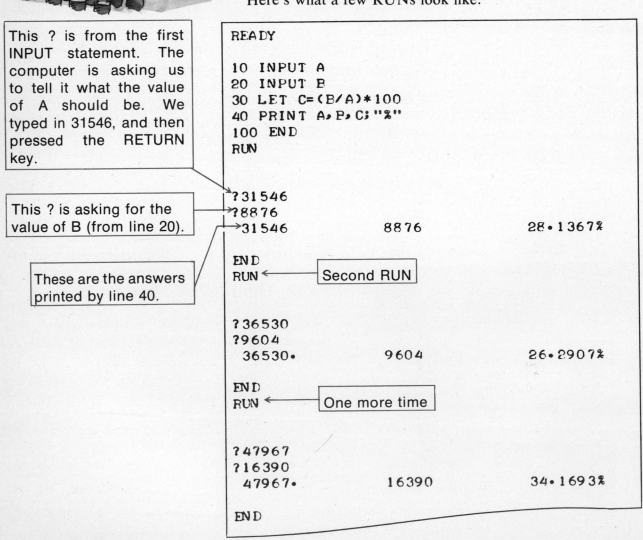

This ? is from the first INPUT statement. The computer is asking us to tell it what the value of A should be. We typed in 31546, and then pressed the RETURN key.

This ? is asking for the value of B (from line 20).

These are the answers printed by line 40.

```
READY

10  INPUT A
20  INPUT B
30  LET C=(B/A)*100
40  PRINT A,B,C;"%"
100 END
RUN

?31546
?8876
 31546          8876          28·1367%

END
RUN ←  Second RUN

?36530
?9604
 36530·         9604          26·2907%

END
RUN ←  One more time

?47967
?16390
 47967·        16390          34·1693%

END
```

Let's summarize the effect of a statement like:

    10 INPUT A

When the computer executes the program and gets to statement 10, it

● prints a ? and then

● waits for you to type in a number for A, followed by a carriage RETURN (you're INPUTting the number into the computer).

OK; that's the basic program in BASIC. Let's spruce it up a bit. First, you know what A, B, and C stand for, the network president knows what they stand for, but not everyone does. So let's put in a few PRINT statements to clear this up. Let's also show the time slot numbers:

```
READY

1 PRINT "TYPE IN THE TIME SLOT NUMBER:"
3 INPUT N
5 PRINT "INPUT THE TOTAL NUMBER OF VIEWERS:"
10 INPUT A
15 PRINT "TYPE IN THE NUMBER OF ABS VIEWERS:"
20 INPUT B
30 LET C=(B/A)*100
35 PRINT "TIME SLOT NO.","TOTAL VIEWERS","VIEWERS OF ABS",
36 PRINT " % WATCHING ABS"
40 PRINT N,A,B,C;"%"
100 END
RUN


TYPE IN THE TIME SLOT NUMBER:
?1
INPUT THE TOTAL NUMBER OF VIEWERS:
?31546
TYPE IN THE NUMBER OF ABS VIEWERS:
?8876
TIME SLOT NO.    TOTAL VIEWERS    VIEWERS OF ABS    % WATCHING ABS
 1                  31546             8876              28.1367%
```

NOTE: Because of the comma at the end of line 35, the computer prints the OUTPUT from lines 35 and 36 on the same line. A new RUN is needed for the next time slot.

ON-LINE

Code Name: /RAT2/

RUN the preceding program using the data for time slots 2, 3, and 4 given in program /RAT1/, Section 2–3.

Let's take a look at another program that uses the INPUT statement. Suppose that you'd like to calculate how many hours a person has slept in his lifetime (well, why not?). Let's assume that everyone sleeps about 1/3 of the time (8 hours out of 24). And let's take a year as 365 days (disregarding leap years).

Here's a program you might use, with a sample RUN.

```
READY

10 PRINT "HOW MANY YEARS OLD ARE YOU?"
20 INPUT Y
30 LET H=Y*24*365
40 PRINT "HOURS LIVED","HOURS SLEPT"
50 PRINT H,H/3
60 END
RUN


HOW MANY YEARS OLD ARE YOU?
?12
HOURS LIVED        HOURS SLEPT
  105120.            35040.

END
RUN


HOW MANY YEARS OLD ARE YOU?
?THIRTEEN
??13
HOURS LIVED        HOURS SLEPT
  113880.            37960.

END
RUN


HOW MANY YEARS OLD ARE YOU?
?11 1/2
EXTRA INPUT - WARNING ONLY

HOURS LIVED        HOURS SLEPT
  972360.            324120.

END
```

Notice that the INPUT statement caused the computer to PRINT a ? and then stop. The student typed in the number 12 and pressed RETURN.

Let's try again.

The student typed letters instead of numerals. The computer doesn't understand letters; so it typed ?? (some computers type messages like "ILLEGAL CHARACTER").

This it understood!

One more time

Fractions not allowed! The computer took the INPUT as 111 (!) and ignored the /2, giving us a very wrong answer.

40

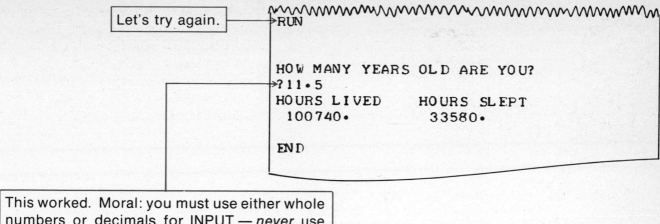

Let's try again.

```
RUN

HOW MANY YEARS OLD ARE YOU?
?11.5
HOURS LIVED        HOURS SLEPT
  100740.            33580.

END
```

This worked. Moral: you must use either whole numbers or decimals for INPUT — *never* use fractions as INPUT.

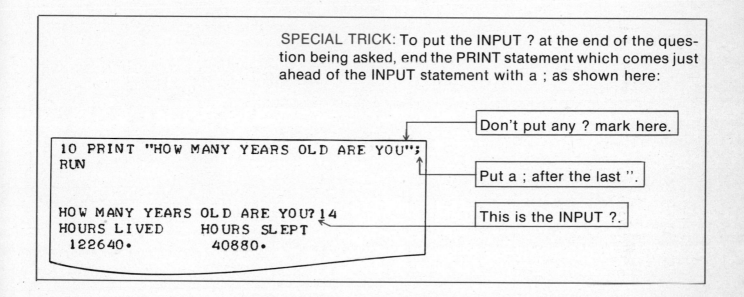

SPECIAL TRICK: To put the INPUT ? at the end of the question being asked, end the PRINT statement which comes just ahead of the INPUT statement with a ; as shown here:

Don't put any ? mark here.

```
10 PRINT "HOW MANY YEARS OLD ARE YOU";
RUN


HOW MANY YEARS OLD ARE YOU?14
HOURS LIVED        HOURS SLEPT
  122640.            40880.
```

Put a ; after the last ".

This is the INPUT ?.

Code Name: /SLEEP/

RUN the preceding program for Y=10, 20, 30, 40, 50, 60. Compare the results for 10 and 30 and for 20 and 60. What do you discover?

Try the program for a variety of ages, including ages like 12.75 (which means 12 3/4 years or 12 years and 9 months old).

Code Name: /RETIRE/

RUN the following program for a variety of values for Y.

ON-LINE

ON-LINE

ON-LINE

```
READY

10 PRINT "HOW MANY YEARS OLD ARE YOU";
20 INPUT Y
30 PRINT "YOU CAN RETIRE IN";65-Y;" YEARS."
40 END
RUN
```

Notice the space between " and YEARS. If we hadn't put it there, the Y in YEARS would be right next to the preceding numeral.

We can use an INPUT statement for several variables. Study this:

```
READY

10 PRINT "TYPE IN THE NO. OF NICKELS, DIMES, AND QUARTERS YOU HAVE:"
20 INPUT N, D, Q
30 PRINT "YOU HAVE"; .05*N+.1*D+.25*Q;" DOLLARS."
40 END
RUN


TYPE IN THE NO. OF NICKELS, DIMES, AND QUARTERS YOU HAVE:
? 3, 5, 4
YOU HAVE 1.65 DOLLARS.
```

Notice that we type in *three* numbers separated by commas to match line 20.

The computer stores the first number in N, the second number in D, and the third number in Q:

N	3
D	5
Q	4

In statement 30 it calculates the dollars you have as shown at the right and then PRINTS the result on the terminal.

```
.05*3= .15
.10*5= .50
.25*4=1.00
      1.65←OUTPUT
```

```
RUN
```
If you forget to type in all the numbers asked for by the program, the computer may keep asking (??) until you do:

```
TYPE IN THE NO. OF NICKELS, DIMES, AND QUARTERS YOU HAVE:
?3
??5, 4
YOU HAVE 1.65 DOLLARS.
```

ON-LINE

Code Name: /MONEY/

RUN the preceding program with different values for N, D, Q.

Code Name: /SUMPROD/

Write and RUN a program that will find both the sum and the product of 4 numbers. Use a statement like:

20 INPUT W,X,Y,Z

SPECIAL INFORMATION ABOUT LARGE NUMBERS

Look at the following program and printout:

```
READY

10 PRINT 30*40*100000
20 END
RUN


1.20000E+08
```

What does 1.20000E+08 mean? It's computer "scientific notation" for 120,000,000 (that's one hundred twenty million). Scientific notation is a shorthand for very large (or very small) numbers. Let's see how it works. First recall that

$$10^2=10\times10=100, \quad 10^3=10\times10\times10=1000, \quad \text{and so on.}$$

This means that

$$1.2\times10^2=120, \quad 1.2\times10^3=1200, \quad \text{and so on.}$$

We can thus see that multiplying 1.2×10^3 is the same as moving the decimal point three places to the right:

$$1.2\times10^3=1200.$$

In the same way, $1.2\times10^8=120000000$. Now you can probably see how scientific notation works:

$1.20000E+08$ means 1.20000×10^8, which means 120000000.

In other words, since a computer can't print 10^8 on a terminal, it uses E+08 to mean $\times10^8$.

The number 8 is called an *exponent,* and E+08 means "times 10 with the exponent positive 8." (The largest possible exponent on the Time Share Corporation system is +38.)

RULE: E+10 means "move the decimal point 10 places to the *right.*"

EXERCISES

Find the missing numbers.

1. (a) $5.00000E+06=$ __5000000__   (b) $8,000,000=$ __?__

2. (a) $8.23000E+08=$ __?__   (b) $27,000,000=2.70000E$ __?__

3. (a) $1.23000E+11=$ __?__   (b) $2,234,000=2.23400E$ __?__

SPECIAL INFORMATION ABOUT SMALL NUMBERS

Look at the following program† and output:

```
READY

10 PRINT ((1/1000)/12)/5280
20 END
RUN


1.57828E-08
```

You can perhaps guess what 1.57828E–08 means. It means

$$1.57828 \times 10^{-8}, \text{ which means } .0000000157828.$$

In case you haven't used negative exponents before, here's how they work:

$$10^{-1} = \frac{1}{10} = .1, \quad 10^{-2} = \frac{1}{10 \times 10} = .01, \quad 10^{-3} = \frac{1}{10 \times 10 \times 10} = .001,$$
and so on.

This means that

$$1.5 \times 10^{-1} = .15, \quad 1.5 \times 10^{-2} = .015, \quad 1.5 \times 10^{-3} = .0015,$$
and so on.

We can thus see that multiplying 1.5×10^{-3} is the same as moving the decimal three places to the left:

$$1.5 \times 10^{-3} = .001.5$$

In our program, 1.57828E–08 means 1.57828×10^{-8}, which means 00000001.57828, or .0000000157828.

RULE: E–10 means "move the decimal point 10 places to the *left*."

EXERCISES

Find the missing numbers.

4. (a) 1.50000E–07 = .00000015   (b) .000000732 = 7.32000E __?__

5. (a) 3.75000E–06 = __?__   (b) .0000006 = __?__

6. (a) 9.82000E–16 = __?__   (b) .00000000000015 = __?__

---

† In case you were wondering, this program finds out how many miles wide a one-thousandth-of-an-inch hair is.

EXERCISES

Supply the missing numbers.

7. (a) $2.00000E+09 = $ ___?___ (b) $2.00000E-09 = $ ___?___
8. (a) $6.30000E+08 = $ ___?___ (b) $6.30000E-08 = $ ___?___
9. (a) $3.14159E+11 = $ ___?___ (b) $3.14159E-11 = $ ___?___
10. (a) ___?___ $= 7000000000$ (b) ___?___ $= 0.000000007$
11. (a) ___?___ $= 328100000000$ (b) ___?___ $= 0.0000003281$
12. (a) ___?___ $= 1000000000$ (b) ___?___ $= 0.00000001$

Code Name: //SUPER-SLEEP//

ON-LINE

Write and RUN a program that prints the number of hours, minutes, and seconds that a person has slept.

Challenge: Can you use your program to find out how old a person has to be in order to have slept a million seconds? a billion seconds?

LET'S REVIEW SECTION 2–4

● The statement

    20 INPUT X

causes the computer to stop, print a ?, and wait for you to type in a decimal number. Then when you press the RETURN key, the computer continues the program, with the number you typed now stored in the location X.

● The statements

    15 PRINT "WHAT IS X";
    20 INPUT X

print WHAT IS X? and wait for you to type in a number.

● The statement

    25 INPUT W,X,Y,Z

causes the computer to stop, print a question mark, and wait for you to type in four numbers, separated by commas. It puts the first number you type in W, the second in X, the third in Y, and the fourth in Z. If you *don't* type four numbers, it will remind you with a double question mark.

● Very large and very small numbers are printed with scientific notation.

EXAMPLES:

    1.34567E+08 means 134567000.
    1.34567E−08 means .0000000134567.

2-5 The GOTO Statement

At last — a statement that allows you to tell the computer where it can go!

Let's illustrate its use in our second TV-rating program (RAT2 in Section 2-4). We'll put in a statement (line 50) that tells the computer to GO (back) TO line 10 and run the program all over again:

```
READY

1 PRINT "TYPE IN THE TIME SLOT NUMBER:"
3 INPUT N
5 PRINT "INPUT THE TOTAL NUMBER OF VIEWERS:"
10 INPUT A
15 PRINT "TYPE IN THE NUMBER OF ABS VIEWERS:"
20 INPUT B
30 LET C=(B/A)*100
35 PRINT "TIME SLOT NO.","TOTAL  VIEWERS","VIEWERS OF ABS",
36 PRINT " % WATCHING ABS"
40 PRINT N, A, B, C; "%"
45 PRINT
50 GO TO 1
100 END
```

Here's the GOTO statement. You may type either
50 GO TO 1
or
50 GOTO 1

Recall that this makes the computer PRINT an empty line and makes the output look nicer.

Now we don't have to continually type RUN. *BUT* — the computer will go eternally back to line 1, through line 50, back to line 1, and so on. This program puts the computer into an "infinite loop." This means that the computer will try to go through a program (or a part of it) forever unless it is stopped.

BEFORE YOU RUN ANY PROGRAM HAVING AN INFINITE LOOP, MAKE SURE YOU KNOW HOW TO STOP THE "RUNNING" (EXECUTION) OF THE PROGRAM. Ask someone how to stop it, or read your computer manual, but make sure you know.

On the Time Share Corporation system, you stop the program execution by pressing and releasing the BREAK key if the program is RUNning; if the computer has printed ? and is waiting for INPUT, you must press CTRL and C at the same time and then press RETURN.

Here's what a RUN of the preceding program would look like:

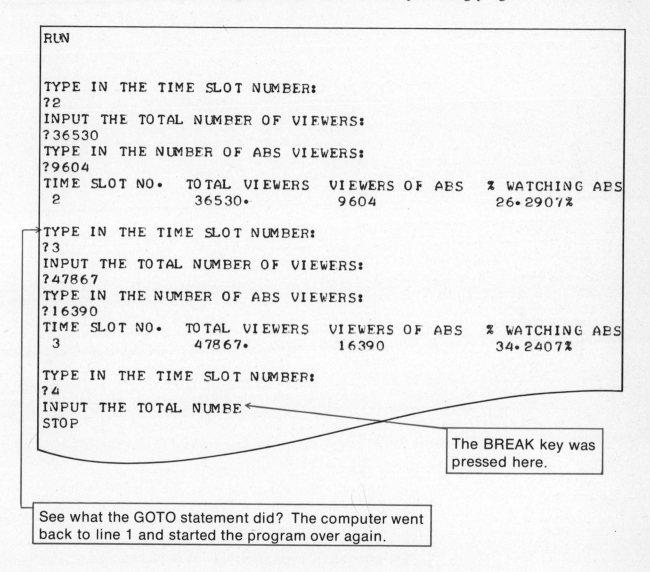

```
RUN


TYPE IN THE TIME SLOT NUMBER:
?2
INPUT THE TOTAL NUMBER OF VIEWERS:
?36530
TYPE IN THE NUMBER OF ABS VIEWERS:
?9604
TIME SLOT NO.    TOTAL VIEWERS   VIEWERS OF ABS   % WATCHING ABS
  2                 36530.           9604             26.2907%

TYPE IN THE TIME SLOT NUMBER:
?3
INPUT THE TOTAL NUMBER OF VIEWERS:
?47867
TYPE IN THE NUMBER OF ABS VIEWERS:
?16390
TIME SLOT NO.    TOTAL VIEWERS   VIEWERS OF ABS   % WATCHING ABS
  3                 47867.          16390            34.2407%

TYPE IN THE TIME SLOT NUMBER:
?4
INPUT THE TOTAL NUMBE
STOP
```

The BREAK key was pressed here.

See what the GOTO statement did? The computer went back to line 1 and started the program over again.

Flow charting is a method of showing in what order the computer will RUN a program. It uses special symbols

INPUT   PRINT   LET   START   END

and a lot of arrows to create a "map" of what the computer will do.

Here's a flow chart of the preceding program:

A FLOW CHART OF THE TV-RATING PROGRAM WITH GOTO

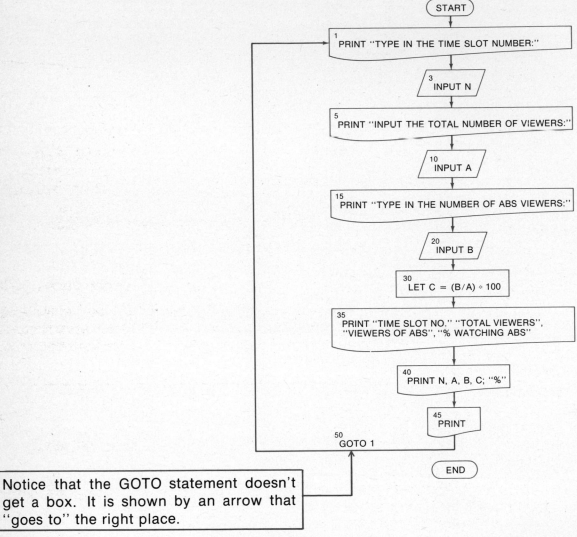

Notice that the GOTO statement doesn't get a box. It is shown by an arrow that "goes to" the right place.

You can see from the flow chart that the computer will never reach the END statement in this particular program, since the line above it represents the GOTO statement. But we still must have an END statement in the program.

Flow charting is especially helpful in planning very complicated programs, since a flow chart makes it easier to follow the logic or sequence of the program.

EXERCISES

Pretend that you are a computer and RUN (on paper) each of these programs.

1. Use 1 for A (STOP after 5 loops):

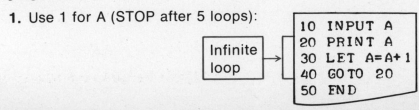

2. Use 1, 2, and 10 for R:

```
10  PRINT "PROGRAM TO FIND AREA OF A CIRCLE"
20  PRINT "TYPE IN RADIUS"
30  INPUT R
40  LET A=3.14159*R*R
50  PRINT "AREA =";A
60  GOTO 20
70  END
```

3. What's wrong with each line of this ''program''?

```
10 INPUT 4              70 INPUT F+G
20 LET B=3A             80 LET H="F+G"
30 INPUT C+A            90 PRINT "H";=H
40 LET C=B+A,          100 GOTO 5
50 INPUT, D,E          110 THE END
60 PRINT "D/E=;D/E
```

Code Name: /RAT3/

There is still one more thing we can do with our television program — shorten it! One way to do this is to input several numbers in one step, as we did in Section 2–4. So, here's our final version:

```
READY

5 PRINT "TYPE, IN THIS ORDER:"
6 PRINT "TIME SLOT NO., TOTAL VIEWERS, VIEWERS OF ABS"
10 INPUT N,A,B
20 LET C=(B/A)*100
30 PRINT "TIME SLOT NO.","TOTAL VIEWERS","VIEWERS OF ABS",
31 PRINT " % WATCHING ABS"
40 PRINT N,A,B,C;"%"
45 PRINT
50 GOTO 6
100 END
RUN
```

We are transferring to line 6, not 5, just to make the output a little shorter.

RUN this program using the information from program /RAT1/, page 36.

SPECIAL: Change line 6 to end with a ; and see what happens.

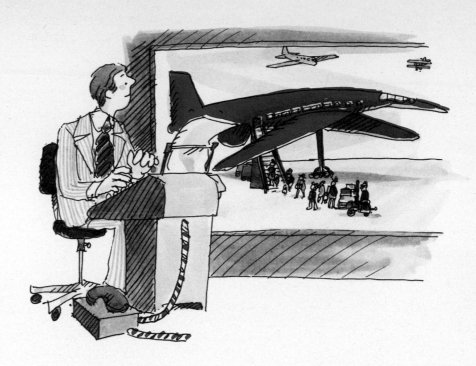

Code Name: //WAU//

You are a dispatch director for TRANS WAUKEGAN AIRLINES. It's your job to give the pilots all the information they need for their flights.

One of the things they have to know is the estimated flight time, that is, how long the flight is expected to take. You're getting tired just guessing — so — in a small step for mankind and a giant leap for Waukegan — you decide to use the computer.

Write and RUN a program using the information given in the table on page 51. Your program should produce OUTPUT like that shown below. (MPH means miles per hour.)

```
RUN


TYPE IN:
FLIGHT NUMBER:?128
PLANE SPEED (MPH):?600
DISTANCE (MILES):?560
WIND SPEED (MPH):?-40

FLIGHT NUMBER: 128
ESTIMATED FLIGHT TIME: 60. MINUTES
FUEL NEEDED: 9960. POUNDS + RESERVE

TYPE IN:
FLIGHT NUMBER:?
```

-40 means a head wind *hindering* the plane's progress. 40 would mean a tail wind *helping* the plane.

Here's some flight information for Trans Waukegan Airlines you can use to test your program.

FLIGHT NO.	PLANE SPEED		DISTANCE (miles)	WIND SPEED (mph)
126	600 mph	BOSTON–PITTSBURGH	483	−45 (head)
381	600 mph	WASHINGTON–LOS ANGELES	2300	−55 (head)
513	600 mph	DENVER–SALT LAKE CITY	371	−25 (head)
125	600 mph	MIAMI–NEW YORK	1092	+38 (tail)
120	600 mph	SAN FRANCISCO–CHICAGO	1858	+50 (tail)
630	600 mph	DETROIT–SEATTLE	1938	−60 (head)
819	600 mph	PHILADELPHIA–WASHINGTON	123	+30 (tail)

ON-LINE   ON-LINE

The speed of the plane with respect to the ground is called the *ground speed.* We are assuming that the wind is either a head wind or a tail wind. If there is a tail wind, the ground speed equals the sum of the plane speed and the wind speed. If there is a head wind, you subtract the wind speed from the plane speed, or you do as the computer does, that is, *add the negative* number representing the head wind speed.

Here are the formulas you'll want to use:

Ground speed in miles per minute=(Plane speed+Wind speed)/60

Time traveled in minutes=Distance (miles)/(Ground speed in miles per minute)

Approx. 166 pounds for each minute of flight time

ON-LINE   ON-LINE   ON-LINE

EXAMPLE

Suppose:

Plane speed=600 MPH

Wind speed=60 MPH (this means a tail wind)

Distance=330 Miles

Then:

Ground speed in miles per minute=

(600+60)/60=660/60=11 Miles per minute

Time traveled in minutes=330/11=30 Minutes

Fuel needed=166*30=4980 Pounds of fuel

LET'S REVIEW SECTION 2–5

● Computers execute statements in the order that is given by the statement line numbers. You can *change* this order by using a GOTO statement. A GOTO statement, as the name implies, will force the computer to go to a specific statement anywhere in a program. For example:

    300 GOTO 179

will force the computer to go from statement 300 to statement 179 and continue execution at that point in the program. We say that the program *branches* to statement 179.

● Several good programming ideas have been illustrated in the last few pages, which we also ought to review:
1. It's a good idea to use a PRINT statement to tell the person RUNning the program what the INPUT statement is asking for.
2. Instead of always reRUNning a program, we can use a GOTO statement to cycle back to the beginning of the program (or to any other point). An even better technique will be shown later.
3. Always label an answer. Don't just say 26.290, for example. Make sure it's clear whether 26.290 is the percent of viewers watching ABS, the weight of your dog, or whatever else you had in mind.

2–6 Statements Using IF . . . THEN ; STOP

Sue is a computer programmer for the transportation department of her state. She has just been given her latest assignment: computerize the automobile driver licensing process. Sue hardly knows where to begin.

But, being logical (all computer programmers are logical), she decides the first thing the computer should do is to look at the person's age and determine what type of license (if any) can possibly be issued. Here is what Sue is thinking:

First, IF the person's age is less than 16, THEN the computer should print:
"NO LICENSE POSSIBLE — UNDER AGE"

But, IF the person is 16, THEN the computer should print:
"JUNIOR OPERATOR'S LICENSE POSSIBLE"

Finally, IF the person is older than 16, THEN the computer should print:
"OPERATOR'S LICENSE POSSIBLE"

Sue has set up three conditions about the applicant's age (by applicant we mean the person who has applied for a driver's license). The conditions are:

(1) the applicant is *younger than 16,* or

(2) the applicant is *16,* or

(3) the applicant is *older than 16.*

One and only one of these conditions can be true for each applicant. Hence, it should be possible to program the computer to find out which fits each applicant. Let's first use English "IF" sentences to show the logical thinking needed to decide which kind of license the applicant can request.

SUPPOSE THAT AN APPLICANT IS 19 YEARS OLD:

(1) IF the applicant is younger than 16, ...
   But the applicant is NOT younger than 16; so condition 1 is FALSE and we continue.

(2) IF the applicant is 16, ...
   But the applicant is NOT 16 years old; so condition 2 is FALSE, and we continue.

(3) IF the applicant is older than 16, ...
   The applicant is 19; so condition 3 is TRUE. We therefore decide that the applicant is eligible for a regular operator's license.

Here's a flow chart that describes our logic:

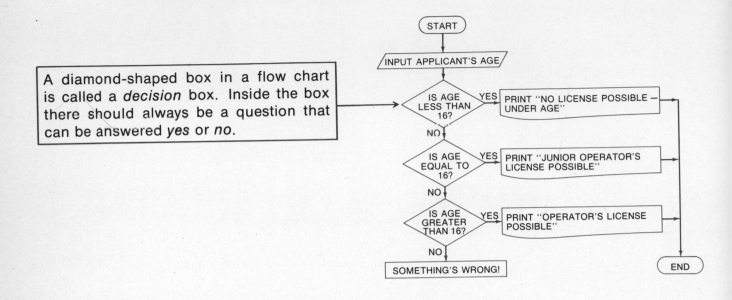

A diamond-shaped box in a flow chart is called a *decision* box. Inside the box there should always be a question that can be answered *yes* or *no*.

Another way to describe a decision box is to say that it corresponds to a condition which is either *true* or *false*. Such conditions are described in BASIC by using the symbols $<$, $=$, or $>$, where:

$A<16$ means A is less than 16

$A=16$ means A is exactly equal to 16

$A>16$ means A is greater than 16

Now, look again at the flow chart. Can you think of an age that gives the answer NO for all three questions in the decision boxes? In other words, can you think of an age which is *not* less than 16, *not* equal to 16, and also *not* greater than 16? Of course not. This tells us that the third decision box is not really needed.

Exercise 1 Redraw the flow chart above so that it uses only two decision boxes.

Before writing her program, Sue decided on one more improvement. Instead of ENDing the program after checking one applicant, she decided to have the program "loop" back to the beginning. But to avoid having an infinite loop, she put in a special decision box at the start which would stop the program anytime she typed in 0 (zero). Her new flow chart is shown at the top of page 55.

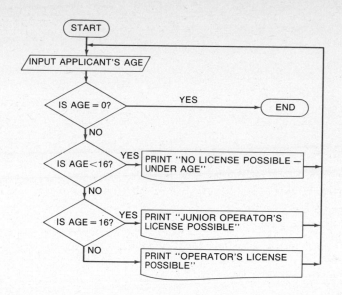

Here's a program based on Sue's flow chart:

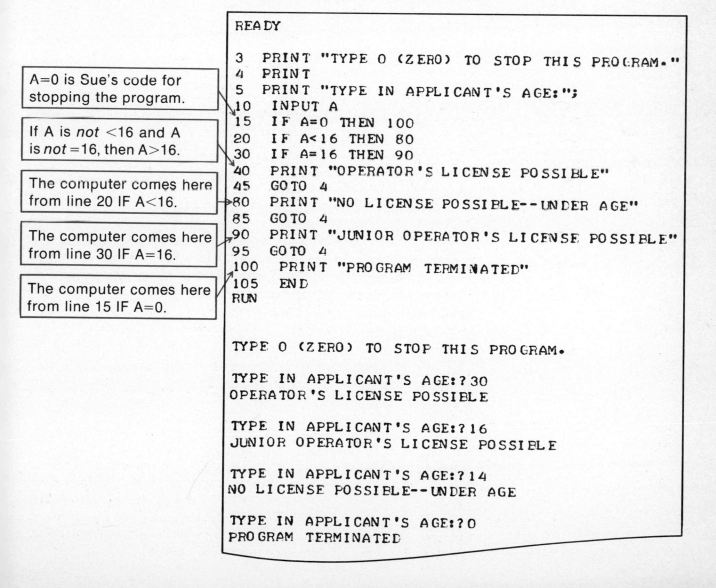

A=0 is Sue's code for stopping the program.

If A is *not* <16 and A is *not* =16, then A>16.

The computer comes here from line 20 IF A<16.

The computer comes here from line 30 IF A=16.

The computer comes here from line 15 IF A=0.

```
READY

3    PRINT "TYPE O (ZERO) TO STOP THIS PROGRAM."
4    PRINT
5    PRINT "TYPE IN APPLICANT'S AGE:";
10   INPUT A
15   IF A=0 THEN 100
20   IF A<16 THEN 80
30   IF A=16 THEN 90
40   PRINT "OPERATOR'S LICENSE POSSIBLE"
45   GOTO 4
80   PRINT "NO LICENSE POSSIBLE--UNDER AGE"
85   GOTO 4
90   PRINT "JUNIOR OPERATOR'S LICENSE POSSIBLE"
95   GOTO 4
100   PRINT "PROGRAM TERMINATED"
105   END
RUN


TYPE O (ZERO) TO STOP THIS PROGRAM.

TYPE IN APPLICANT'S AGE:?30
OPERATOR'S LICENSE POSSIBLE

TYPE IN APPLICANT'S AGE:?16
JUNIOR OPERATOR'S LICENSE POSSIBLE

TYPE IN APPLICANT'S AGE:?14
NO LICENSE POSSIBLE--UNDER AGE

TYPE IN APPLICANT'S AGE:?0
PROGRAM TERMINATED
```

Here are examples of three other kinds of conditions that can be used in BASIC:

A>=16   means   A greater than 16 or A equal to 16
A<=16   means   A less than 16 or A equal to 16
A<>16   means   A *not* equal to 16 (on some computers # can be used instead of <>)

The condition A>=18 is true if either A>18 *or* A=18. Here's an example showing how you might use such a condition. This example also illustrates the use of the key word STOP.

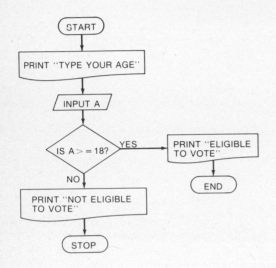

```
10    PRINT "TYPE YOUR AGE."
20    INPUT A
30    IF A >= 18 THEN 60
40    PRINT "NOT ELIGIBLE TO VOTE"
50    STOP
60    PRINT "ELIGIBLE TO VOTE"
70    END
```

USING THE KEY WORD STOP

RULE: The last statement in a BASIC program *must be* an END statement. If you wish a program to stop executing at any other place, use a statement with the key word STOP.

Exercise 2 Here is a part of a program. At the top of page 57, we give you 10 versions of line 40. In each case, decide if the condition is true or false, and indicate the next statement to which the program will "branch."

```
10    LET B=16
20    LET C=24
30    LET D=48
40    -----------
50    -----------
60    -----------
-----------------
```

STATEMENT 40:	CONDITION IS:	BRANCH TO:
1. 40 IF D>B THEN 60	TRUE (48>16)	60
2. 40 IF B=D THEN 60	FALSE (16 is not equal to 48)	50
3. 40 IF B/8=D/C THEN 60	TRUE WHY?	60
4. 40 IF B<>D THEN 60	? WHY?	?
5. 40 IF D<=2*C THEN 60	TRUE WHY?	?
6. 40 IF D/B>=D/C THEN 80	? WHY?	?
7. 40 IF 3*D<>2*B THEN 80	? WHY?	?
8. 40 IF B*D<=C*D THEN 80	? WHY?	?
9. 40 IF C+B<40 THEN 80	? WHY?	?
10. 40 IF B*B>=D*D THEN 80	? WHY?	?

Exercise 3 Pretend you are a computer and simulate running the following program. It is a ridiculous program, but it is an interesting puzzle. If you do it right, you'll receive a pleasant surprise. (If all else fails, try it on a computer.)

```
10    LET F=10
20    IF 18<2*F THEN 40
30    PRINT "WAS"
35    GOTO 140
40    LET G=20
50    IF G/F <> 4/2 THEN 70
60    PRINT "THIS"
70    GOTO 90
80    PRINT "NEVER"
83    PRINT "A"
85    GOTO 60
90    PRINT "PROGRAM"
100   LET F=F-7
110   IF F/2 <= 1.5 THEN 20
120   PRINT "EVER"
130   IF F/2>1.5 THEN 70
140   PRINT "RUN"
150   IF G+F<25 THEN 165
157   PRINT "SPOT"
158   PRINT "RUN"
160   LET F=F+1
165   IF G-F <= F+F THEN 157
170   PRINT "CORRECTLY."
180   END
```

PROGRAM WAS RUN CORRECTLY

Code Name: /MATHQUIZ/

Here is a program that is short, yet it gives a long addition quiz (twenty questions). Draw a flow chart and then RUN it. (You might also try changing it to a multiplication quiz.)

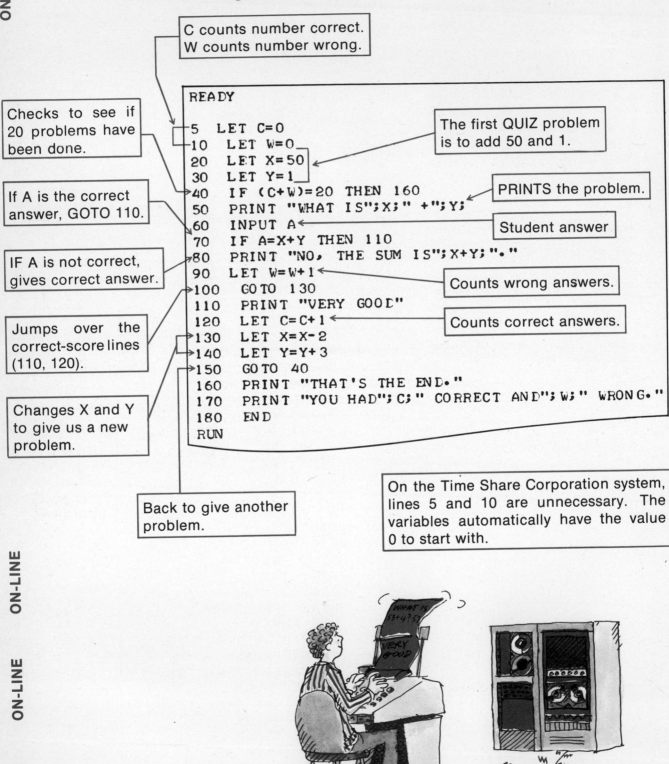

C counts number correct.
W counts number wrong.

Checks to see if 20 problems have been done.

If A is the correct answer, GOTO 110.

IF A is not correct, gives correct answer.

Jumps over the correct-score lines (110, 120).

Changes X and Y to give us a new problem.

Back to give another problem.

The first QUIZ problem is to add 50 and 1.

PRINTS the problem.

Student answer

Counts wrong answers.

Counts correct answers.

```
READY

5    LET C=0
10   LET W=0
20   LET X=50
30   LET Y=1
40   IF (C+W)=20 THEN 160
50   PRINT "WHAT IS";X;" +";Y;
60   INPUT A
70   IF A=X+Y THEN 110
80   PRINT "NO, THE SUM IS";X+Y;"."
90   LET W=W+1
100  GO TO 130
110  PRINT "VERY GOOD"
120  LET C=C+1
130  LET X=X-2
140  LET Y=Y+3
150  GO TO 40
160  PRINT "THAT'S THE END."
170  PRINT "YOU HAD";C;" CORRECT AND";W;" WRONG."
180  END
RUN
```

On the Time Share Corporation system, lines 5 and 10 are unnecessary. The variables automatically have the value 0 to start with.

Let's discuss another use of the IF . . . THEN statement. Suppose that we wish to print the squares of all the whole numbers from 1 to 10. (The square of 2 is 2×2, or 4.) We could say:

```
10 PRINT 1*1
20 PRINT 2*2
30 PRINT 3*3
        .
        .        ← There would be 6 additional state-
        .          ments here.
100 PRINT 10*10
110 END
```

But that's rather ridiculous! We can write a much shorter program which will do the same thing, as shown in the following flow chart and program.

FLOW CHART

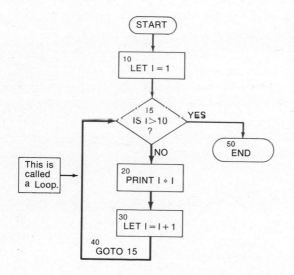

PROGRAM

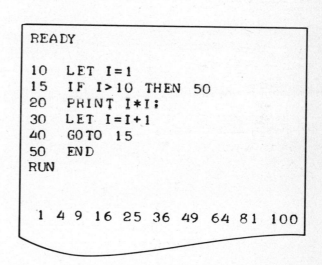

```
READY

10   LET I=1
15   IF I>10 THEN 50
20   PRINT I*I;
30   LET I=I+1
40   GOTO 15
50   END
RUN

  1  4 9  16 25 36 49 64 81 100
```

Notice that the program would be the same length if we decided to print the squares of the whole numbers from 1 to 100!

You can see from the flow chart that the program automatically repeats itself. This is called *looping*.

On the next page we shall examine this program in detail.

Sets the first (initial) value of I. Since we want the numbers 1 to 10, we set I equal to 1 for a start.

We first check to see if I has gone past 10. If it has, we want line 50 (END). If not, we wish to PRINT I∗I, as in line 20.

After the square of a number is printed, we then want to increment (increase) I by 1 to get the *next* number.

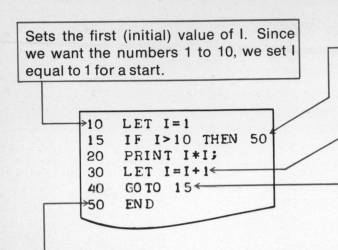

```
10    LET I=1
15    IF I>10 THEN 50
20    PRINT I*I;
30    LET I=I+1
40    GO TO 15
50    END
```

Then we branch back to statement 15, where we decide whether or not to continue.

The END statement is reached only when I exceeds 10.

Step 15 uses IF . . . THEN to *test* if we are finished. We put our test right at the start of this program. (It is also possible to put it other places.) Notice that IF . . . THEN provides a neat way of escaping from a loop. In other words, there won't be an "infinite" loop.

SUMMARY: Programs can avoid infinite loops by using IF . . . THEN statements together with statements that *increment* the loop variable.

It's something like a bus driver who travels the "loop" shown below, over and over. Each time he passes the starting point, he pushes the button to *increment* his trip counter. He gets out of the loop and heads for the garage when his counter shows >10 trips.

ON-LINE

Code Name: /SEQ/

Change the preceding program to print out the squares of the numbers from 10 to 30.

ON-LINE

Write (OFF-LINE) a QUIZ program on any subject (music, history, physics, mathematics, accounting, and so on) that appeals to you. You can use the following program as an example. Your program should be at least as long, and it should keep score. Include enough directions so that anyone can RUN your program. When you are sure it's ready, try it ON-LINE with a friend.

SAMPLE QUIZ PROGRAM (sample RUN is given on page 62):

```
READY

5    LET S=0
10   PRINT "HERE IS A LIST OF SIX NAMES IN MUSIC.  YOU WILL BE"
11   PRINT "ASKED FOUR QUESTIONS; ANSWER EACH WITH THE NUMBER"
12   PRINT "CORRESPONDING TO THE CORRECT NAME."
15   PRINT "1. BEATLES              2. ENRICO CARUSO"
17   PRINT "3. BOB DYLAN            4. LUDWIG VAN BEETHOVEN"
20   PRINT "5. JOHANN S. BACH       6. LOUIS ARMSTRONG"
25   PRINT
30   PRINT "WHO WROTE NINE SYMPHONIES?"
40   INPUT A
50   IF A=4 THEN 64
60   PRINT "NO, BEETHOVEN (4) IS THE ANSWER."
63   GOTO 70
64   LET S=S+1
65   PRINT "RIGHT!"
70   PRINT "NAME A FORMER MAJOR 'ROCK' GROUP."
80   INPUT B
90   IF B=1 THEN 104
100  PRINT "NO, BEATLES (1) IS THE ANSWER."
103  GOTO 110
104  LET S=S+1
105  PRINT "CORRECT!"
110  PRINT "A FAMOUS ITALIAN OPERA STAR WHO DIED IN 1921 WAS:"
120  INPUT C
130  IF C=2 THEN 144
140  PRINT "NO, ENRICO CARUSO (2) IS THE ANSWER."
143  GOTO 150
144  LET S=S+1
145  PRINT "YES!!"
150  PRINT "WHO WAS 'SATCHMO'?"
160  INPUT D
170  IF D=6 THEN 184
180  PRINT "NO, LOUIS ARMSTRONG (6) IS THE ANSWER."
183  GOTO 190
184  LET S=S+1
185  PRINT "GREAT!"
190  PRINT "OK, YOUR SCORE OUT OF A POSSIBLE 4 IS"; S; "."
200  IF S=4 THEN 220
210  PRINT "HOPE YOU HAD FUN.  MAYBE NEXT TIME YOU CAN DO BETTER."
215  STOP
220  PRINT "YOU HAD A PERFECT SCORE.  CONGRATULATIONS!!!"
230  END
```

Here is a sample RUN of the QUIZ program shown on page 61:

```
RUN

HERE IS A LIST OF SIX NAMES IN MUSIC.  YOU WILL BE
ASKED FOUR QUESTIONS; ANSWER EACH WITH THE NUMBER
CORRESPONDING TO THE CORRECT NAME.
1. BEATLES            2. ENRICO CARUSO
3. BOB DYLAN          4. LUDWIG VAN BEETHOVEN
5. JOHANN S. BACH     6. LOUIS ARMSTRONG


WHO WROTE NINE SYMPHONIES?
?5
NO, BEETHOVEN (4) IS THE ANSWER.
NAME A FORMER MAJOR 'ROCK' GROUP.
?1
CORRECT!
A FAMOUS ITALIAN OPERA STAR WHO DIED IN 1921 WAS:
?5
NO, ENRICO CARUSO (2) IS THE ANSWER.
WHO WAS 'SATCHMO'?
?6
GREAT!
OK, YOUR SCORE OUT OF A POSSIBLE 4 IS 2.
HOPE YOU HAD FUN.  MAYBE NEXT TIME YOU CAN DO BETTER.
```

LET'S REVIEW SECTION 2-6

● The IF . . . THEN statement is one of the most important statements in programming. It allows a computer program to *decide* whether the next statement to be executed is the one right below, or the one which the THEN part mentions. Some examples of correct IF . . . THEN statements are shown at the right. The parts of the IF . . . THEN statement are:

23 IF A<4 THEN 200
97 IF C>=9*A THEN 320
126 IF R=S+T THEN 560
516 IF V<>M+I THEN 680

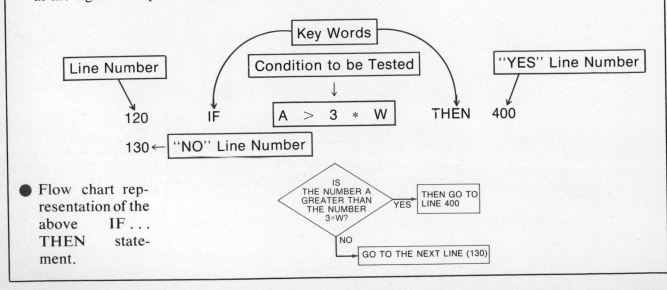

● Flow chart representation of the above IF . . . THEN statement.

2-7 Statements Using the Key Words FOR and NEXT ; STEP

The FOR and NEXT statements were invented to simplify the writing of programs that do the same kind of thing over and over again — in other words programs that contain loops. This means that FOR and NEXT can help you write short programs that produce lots of output.

The IF . . . THEN statement can also be used to write programs with loops (see page 59), but using FOR and NEXT is easier in those cases to which it applies. Let's compare using the two methods to print the squares of the first ten natural numbers:

Looping with IF . . . THEN	Looping with FOR and NEXT
10 LET I = 1 20 IF I > 10 THEN 60 30 PRINT I * I 40 LET I = I + 1 50 GOTO 20 60 END	10 FOR I = 1 TO 10 20 PRINT I * I 30 NEXT I 40 END

These two programs do the same thing:

● They both start I out equal to 1.

● They both PRINT I*I, and then increase I by 1.

● They both continue to run *over and over* until finally I reaches 10.

● Then they both stop.

In other words, both of these programs would RUN as shown at the left.

```
RUN


  1
  4
  9
 16
 25
 36
 49
 64
 81
100
```

Notice that FOR and NEXT are *both* used in the second program. They are always used as a pair.

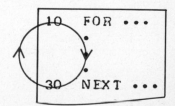

We can see the "loop" in the first program (the one that uses IF . . . THEN) by drawing a flow chart. We can also see that when the number I gets larger than 10, the IF statement will throw the computer out of the loop.

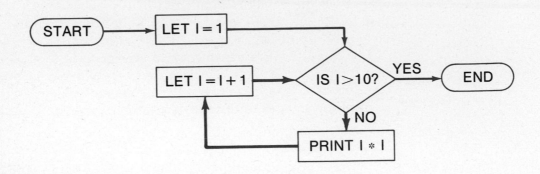

The heavy colored lines show where the looping takes place.

This looping idea works the same way in a FOR-NEXT loop, except that the computer automatically does the

incrementing step   (LET I=I+1)

and the

testing step   (IS I>10?).

Here's a description of the FOR-NEXT version of the same program.

BASIC	ENGLISH

`10    FOR I=1 TO 10`
`20    PRINT I*I`
`30    NEXT I`
`40    END`
	Let I=1, print I*I,
	
	go back and get the next I(=2), print I*I,
	
	go back and get the next I(=3), print I*I,
	
	and so on,
	
	until we have finally printed I*I for I=10.

Are you confused? The above explanation of FOR-NEXT loops is from a computer viewpoint. Let's look at FOR-NEXT loops from a human viewpoint.

Let's write a "program" to describe what really happens when a person does something several times. For example, suppose that we want someone to clap his hands five times.

A "program" that we might try on him is the following:

1. FOR each number from 1 to 5, you're going to do something. Let's start with 1.
2. Clap your hands.
3. Go back and get the NEXT number, but stop if the next number is greater than 5.

Someone following our "program" would do the following:

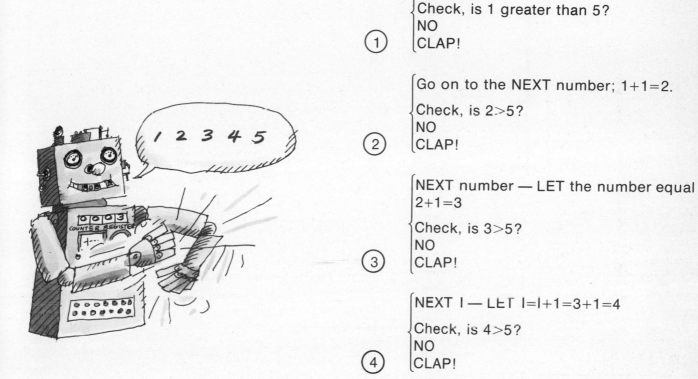

① Start with 1.
Check, is 1 greater than 5?
NO
CLAP!

② Go on to the NEXT number; 1+1=2.
Check, is 2>5?
NO
CLAP!

③ NEXT number — LET the number equal 2+1=3
Check, is 3>5?
NO
CLAP!

④ NEXT I — LET I=I+1=3+1=4
Check, is 4>5?
NO
CLAP!

⑤ NEXT I — LET I=I+1=4+1=5
Check is 5>5?
NO
CLAP!

NEXT I — LET I=I+1=5+1=6
Check, is 6>5?
YES
STOP!

If you felt that the above was silly for human beings, we agree. That's because human beings are much more intelligent than computers. But now you have some idea of how FOR and NEXT work.

SUMMARY: The FOR and NEXT statements are used to count for the computer while it does something over and over.

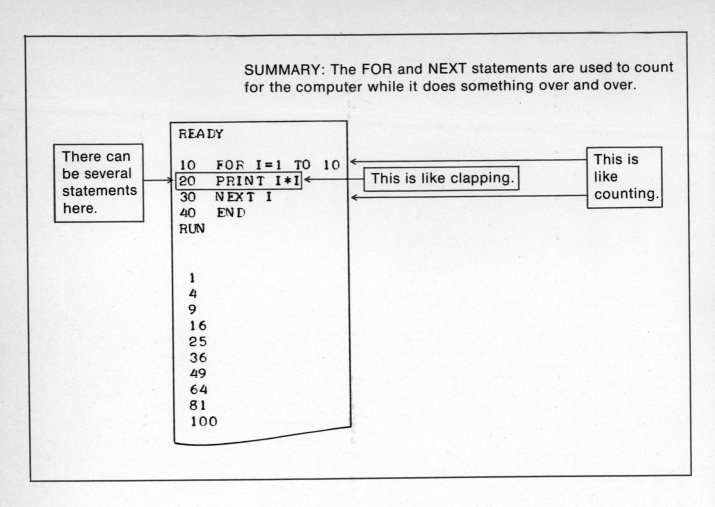

There can be several statements here.

```
READY

10    FOR I=1 TO 10
20    PRINT I*I
30    NEXT I
40    END
RUN

      1
      4
      9
      16
      25
      36
      49
      64
      81
      100
```

This is like clapping.

This is like counting.

Here's an example which has 4 statements *between* the FOR and NEXT statements. These 4 statements are called the *body* of the loop.

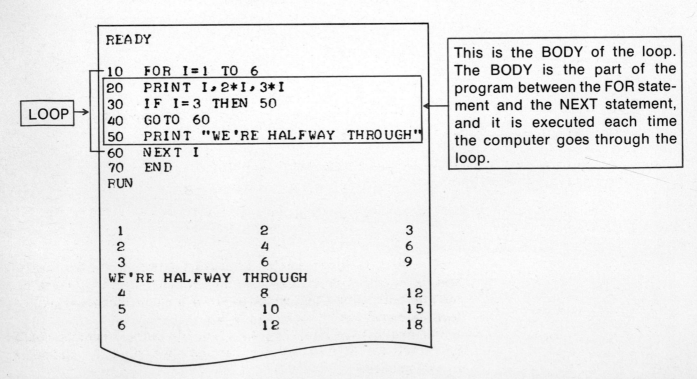

```
READY

10    FOR I=1 TO 6
20    PRINT I,2*I,3*I
30    IF I=3 THEN 50
40    GOTO 60
50    PRINT "WE'RE HALFWAY THROUGH"
60    NEXT I
70    END
RUN

      1              2              3
      2              4              6
      3              6              9
WE'RE HALFWAY THROUGH
      4              8              12
      5              10             15
      6              12             18
```

LOOP

This is the BODY of the loop. The BODY is the part of the program between the FOR statement and the NEXT statement, and it is executed each time the computer goes through the loop.

A FOR statement doesn't have to start with 1. Look at the following:

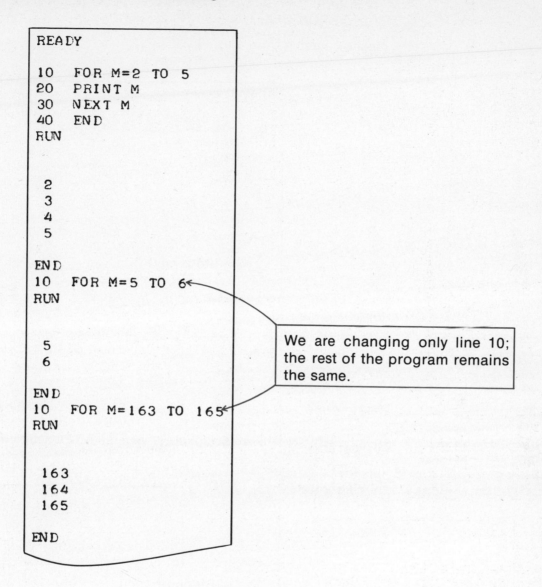

```
READY

10    FOR M=2 TO 5
20    PRINT M
30    NEXT M
40    END
RUN


2
3
4
5

END
10    FOR M=5 TO 6
RUN


5
6

END
10    FOR M=163 TO 165
RUN


163
164
165

END
```

We are changing only line 10; the rest of the program remains the same.

If you were told to count to 10 by 2's, you would say:

    2   4   6   8   10

How about counting from 1 to 9 by 2's:

    1   3   5   7   9

Or count from 2 to 11 by 4's:

    2   6   10.

Note that the lower number (1 in from *1* to 9) is the first value, and the number you are counting "by" is then *added* to it to get the next number. You again check to see if the new number is greater than the upper limit (9 in from 1 to *9*).

In counting from 2 to 11 by 4's, (2, 6, 10), the next number would have been 14; but 14 is greater than the upper limit, 11, and so, it is *not* included.

We can include a similar idea in the FOR statement by using the additional key word STEP.

FOR Z=1 TO 7 STEP 2

means counting from 1 to 7 by 2's.

```
READY

10    FOR Z=1 TO 7 STEP 2
20    PRINT Z
30    NEXT Z
40    END
RUN


1 ⎫
3 ⎬ Steps of 2
5 ⎪
7 ⎭

END
10    FOR Z=2 TO 11 STEP 4
RUN


2  ⎫
6  ⎬ Steps of 4
10 ⎭

END
10    FOR Z=0 TO 50 STEP 10
RUN


0  ⎫
10 ⎪
20 ⎬ Steps of 10
30 ⎪
40 ⎪
50 ⎭

END
```

NOTE: Unless there is a STEP part in the FOR statement, the computer assumes the values are to be *increased by 1*. 10 FOR I=1 TO 4 *means the same as* 10 FOR I=1 TO 4 STEP 1.

Here's an example of "stepping backward"!

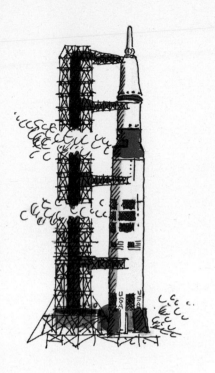

```
READY

10    FOR Z=10 TO 0 STEP -1
20    PRINT Z
30    NEXT Z
40    PRINT "***********BLAST-OFF***********"
50    END
RUN


 10
 9
 8
 7
 6
 5
 4
 3
 2
 1
 0
***********BLAST-OFF***********
```

Notice that when you are "stepping backward," the larger number in the FOR statement comes first:

FOR Z=⑩ TO 0 STEP −1

On the other hand, when you are "stepping forward," the larger number comes second:

FOR I=2 TO ⑪ STEP 3

Really, then, we can say that each FOR statement determines a set of values for a particular variable:

10 FOR F=1 TO 3

determines the set {1,2,3} for the variable F.

10 FOR P=2 TO 8 STEP 2

determines the set {2,4,6,8} for the variable P.

Exercise 1 For each FOR statement, write the set of values that will be used:

FOR Statement	Variable	Set of Values
FOR L=3 TO 9 STEP 3	L	{3,6,9}
FOR G=1 TO 9 STEP 2	G	{1,3,5,7,9}
FOR Y2=3 TO 8 STEP 3	?	?
FOR W=314 TO 817 STEP 200	?	?
FOR B7=3 TO 16 STEP 5	?	?
FOR R=1 TO 6	?	?
FOR M8=3 TO 27 STEP 6	?	?

Exercise 2 Now, given a variable and a set of values, write an appropriate FOR statement.

Variable	Set of Values	FOR Statement
Q	{1,4,7,10}	FOR Q=1 TO 10 STEP 3
P	{18,25,32,39,46}	?
K3	{200,201,202,203,204}	?
X	{1,1.1,1.2,1.3,1.4,1.5,1.6,1.7}	?
N4	{10,8,6,4,2}	?
D6	{3,8,13,18,23,28}	?

Look at the following programs and then answer the questions after each program.

Exercise 3

```
10   FOR P=8 TO 30 STEP 6
20   PRINT "HELLO"
30   NEXT P
40   PRINT "GOOD-BYE"
50   END
```

How many HELLO's will be printed?
How many GOOD-BYE's will be printed?

Exercise 4

```
10   FOR L=3 TO 19 STEP 4
20   PRINT L-2
30   PRINT L+2
40   NEXT L
50   END
```

How many numbers will be printed in all?
Now, print the numbers out.

Exercise 5 Find the two errors in the following "program":

```
10 FOR F=36 TO 34 STEP 2
20 PRINT F
30 NEXT G
40 END
```

USING VARIABLES IN FOR-NEXT STATEMENTS

Here's a simple program that will print out 5 rows of 10 asterisks each:

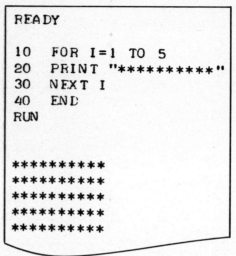

```
READY

10   FOR I=1 TO 5
20   PRINT "**********"
30   NEXT I
40   END
RUN


**********
**********
**********
**********
**********
```

That's simple enough! Now, let's change the above program as follows:

```
5 INPUT R
10 FOR I=1 TO R
```

With this change, we can have different numbers of rows printed out. Watch:

```
RUN


?3
**********
**********
**********

END
RUN


?4
**********
**********
**********
**********
```

Since R=3, line 10 becomes

        10 FOR I=1 TO 3

and 3 rows of asterisks are printed.

Since R=4, line 10 becomes

        10 FOR I=1 TO 4

and 4 rows of asterisks are printed.

Now that we know that we can put a variable in a FOR statement, let's change the program again:

```
READY

5    PRINT "HOW MANY BLOCKS OF ASTERISKS DO YOU WANT";
6    INPUT T
10   FOR H=1 TO T
15   PRINT "HOW MANY ROWS OF ASTERISKS DO YOU WANT IN BLOCK";H;
20   INPUT R
25   FOR I=1 TO R
30   PRINT "**********"
35   NEXT I
40   NEXT H
50   END
```

The preceding program illustrates NESTED FOR LOOPS. As the name implies, NESTED LOOPS are loops nested, or included, within other loops. In the above program, we have the FOR-NEXT loop with H, and within *that* loop, the FOR-NEXT loop with I. The two loops work like this:

(Leaving out the other steps.)

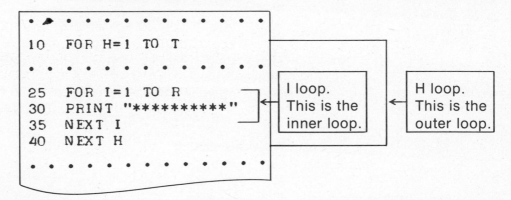

```
10   FOR H=1 TO T


25   FOR I=1 TO R
30   PRINT "**********"
35   NEXT I
40   NEXT H
```

I loop. This is the inner loop.

H loop. This is the outer loop.

When the computer reaches the FOR statement in line 10, it sets H=1 and then continues, as usual, executing the *body* of that loop. But it just so happens that the body of the H loop is another FOR-NEXT loop — the I loop. So the computer now must go through the body of the I loop, over and over until I is greater than R (the number of rows of asterisks wanted).

When I is greater than R, the computer skips to the line right after the NEXT I, just as it would in any FOR loop. The line the computer skipped to is the NEXT H which returns the computer to line 10 (finally!). Now it sets H=2 and repeats the whole process again.

You might compare this with the way an odometer on an automobile works. The tenth-mile dial must go through all the ten digits *before* the mile dial moves one digit.

The best way to understand what a computer does with nested FOR loops is to RUN the program and study the output. Here is a sample RUN:

```
RUN


HOW MANY BLOCKS OF ASTERISKS DO YOU WANT? 3
HOW MANY ROWS OF ASTERISKS DO YOU WANT IN BLOCK 1? 4
**********
**********
**********
**********
HOW MANY ROWS OF ASTERISKS DO YOU WANT IN BLOCK 2? 2
**********
**********
HOW MANY ROWS OF ASTERISKS DO YOU WANT IN BLOCK 3? 6
**********
**********
**********
**********
**********
**********
```

Do you see that the computer went through the H loop 3 times? And, that each time the H loop was executed, the I loop was run first 4, then 2, and finally 6 times? If you keep in mind that the BODY of the H loop IS the I loop, this is easier to understand.

EXERCISES

Run each program BY HAND.

1.

```
10    PRINT "THIS IS A COMPUTER."
20    FOR K=1 TO 4
30    PRINT "NOTHING CAN GO"
40    FOR J=1 TO 3
50    PRINT "WRONG"
60    NEXT J
70    NEXT K
80    END
```

2.

```
10    FOR W=2 TO 8 STEP 2
20    PRINT "*    *    *"
30    FOR X=18 TO 20
40    PRINT "  *    *"
50    NEXT X
60    NEXT W
70    END
```

(Now you'll understand Program 1 in Section 1–10.)

A SPECIAL TRICK

You know that using the semicolon (;) at the end of a PRINT statement (so that the computer does not give a new line feed) can create interesting effects. We can use this idea in printing out rows of asterisks.

Here the semicolon caused the 5 asterisks to be printed on the same line.

EXERCISES

Run each program by hand, and show the OUTPUT.

3.

```
10    FOR I=8 TO 10
20    FOR J=13 TO 18
30    PRINT "*";
40    NEXT J
50    PRINT
60    NEXT I
70    END
```

←will print out __?__ lines.
←will put __?__ asterisks on each line.

←We need this PRINT statement to tell the computer NOT to continue to print on the same line. Instead, we want a new line.

4.

```
10    FOR S=1 TO 10
20    FOR T=1 TO S
30    PRINT "*";
40    NEXT T
50    PRINT
60    NEXT S
70    END
```

ON-LINE

Code Name: /STARS/

RUN the program in Exercise 2.

Code Name: /TRIANGLE/

RUN the program in Exercise 4.

ON-LINE

Code Name: /BLOCKS/

Write and RUN a program that will print 3 rectangles, each having 4 rows of 7 asterisks each, using nested loops.

Code Name: //GRADE//

Write a program (OFF-LINE) that plots a bar graph of the grades on a quiz. After you have perfected your program, try it ON-LINE. The output might look like this, where each unit is represented by <*>.

```
RUN


INPUT GRADES.   TYPE 101 WHEN FINISHED.
?85
?90
?100
?95
?85
?55
?100
?75
?60
?75
?20
?40
?65
?70
?75
?101

GRADES              DISTRIBUTION
0 TO 20             <*>
21 TO 40            <*>
41 TO 60            <*><*>
61 TO 80            <*><*><*><*><*>
81 TO 100           <*><*><*><*><*><*>

AVERAGE GRADE WAS 72.6667
```

If you need some ideas, try running this experimental program.

```
READY

1 PRINT "INPUT GRADES. ";
2 PRINT " TYPE 101 TO STOP."
5 LET T=0
10 INPUT G
20 IF G>100 THEN 150
25 IF G<70 THEN 10
30 LET T=T+1
40 GOTO 10
150 PRINT "70 TO 100",
200 FOR K=1 TO T
300 PRINT "<*>";
400 NEXT K
500 END
```

ON-LINE

Write a program (OFF-LINE) to solve the following problem. Then RUN it ON-LINE.

You are an engineer helping to design a new type of amusement park ride. The layout looks like this:

The car starts to the left of point A with a certain starting speed. Then it continues along the track, passing "booster" stations A, B, C, D, then A, B, C, D again, and so on. Every time the car passes station A, B, C, or D, its speed is increased 10% by the gear you see rotating below the track. If, for instance, the car is traveling at 5 miles per hour coming into station B, when it leaves B, it will be traveling at 5+.1*5=5.5 miles per hour.

The ride is designed so that the car goes around 10 times before the power is cut and the car coasts to a halt. The designers are unsure as to what speed the car should start. Some say 2 miles per hour, others say 5 miles per hour. To end their dilemma, they turn to you.

STARTING SPEED (miles/hour)	FINAL SPEED (after 10th trip around)
.5	?
1.0	?
1.5	?
2.0	?
2.5	?
3.0	?
3.5	?
4.0	?
4.5	?
5.0	?
5.5	?
6.0	?

Well, now that you're stuck with the job, what are you going to do? Probably the best idea would be to make a chart of the various starting speeds of the car, and, for each starting speed, show what the final speed of the car would be. Thus, you want to write a program to complete the table shown at the left.

HINTS: You will need NESTED FOR LOOPS.
The OUTER LOOP will control the increasing starting speed.
   (FOR S=.5 TO 6 STEP .5)
The INNER LOOP will calculate the speed after 40 "boosts."
   (FOR B=1 TO 40)

SAMPLE CALCULATION

Suppose that the starting speed were 10 mph:

BOOST NO.	SPEED AFTER BOOST
1	Speed=10+.1*10=11
2	Speed=11+.1*11=12.1
3	Speed=12.1+.1*12.1=13.31
.	and so on, for 40 boosts. The reason that
.	we use 40 is that we go around the track 10
.	times, passing 4 booster stations each time.
40	

LET'S REVIEW SECTION 2–7

● FOR-NEXT loops are used for repetitive calculations or *looping*. There are several parts to a FOR-NEXT loop. The loop starts with a *FOR* statement at the beginning, and ends with a *NEXT* statement at the end.

● A variable is chosen as a counter (for example, I), and lower and upper values are specified for it. A STEP part is sometimes also included to show how much I should be increased each time the loop is repeated. For example:

10 FOR I=10 TO 16 STEP 2

| First value | Second value | Step value |

Thus line 10 says that I will be taken from the set of numbers {10, 12, 14, 16}.
At the end of the loop, a NEXT statement is always needed. The general format for a FOR-NEXT loop is:

```
10 FOR I=A TO B
20
30  BODY OF LOOP
40 NEXT I
```

● Nested loops are loops within loops:

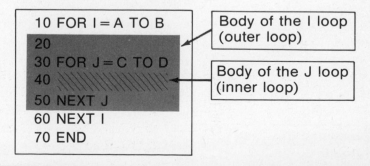

```
10 FOR I = A TO B
20
30 FOR J = C TO D
40
50 NEXT J
60 NEXT I
70 END
```

Body of the I loop (outer loop)

Body of the J loop (inner loop)

2–8 Storing Programs on Paper Tape

> NOTE: This section is *not* about computer programming. It tells you how to use a special piece of equipment called the *paper tape punch and reader.* You can read through this section at any time to get the general idea, and then refer to it whenever you wish to use paper tape.

Why paper tape? As you move along in the computer programming world, your programs are bound to get longer and longer. When that happens, having to type in the same program more than once (say on different days) becomes discouraging. It would be nice if we could "store" our programs for future use, and then later have the machine type in our programs for us. That's exactly what paper tape can do. Let's see how.

If your terminal is equipped to punch paper tapes, it may be of the type shown in the photograph. The combination paper tape *punch* and *reader* is on the left side of the terminal. The *punch* has a narrow yellow paper tape unrolling under a panel of four buttons marked ON, OFF, BSP, and REL. The *reader* is the part in front with the small plastic cover.

This machine *stores* programs for us by *punching* holes in the paper tape.

A punched tape looks like this:

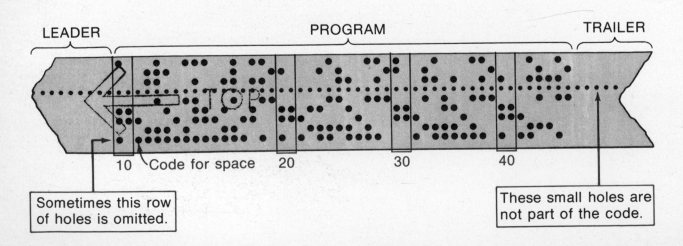

LEADER PROGRAM TRAILER

10 Code for space 20 30 40

Sometimes this row of holes is omitted.

These small holes are not part of the code.

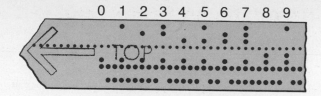

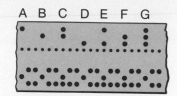

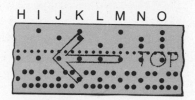

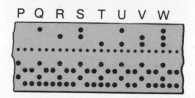

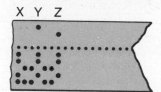

Each vertical line is a code for one of the characters used on a terminal. You don't have to know these codes — they are automatically "decoded" back into letters, numerals, and other symbols when the tape is "read" by the *tape reader*. The picture at the left shows you some of the codes. (We've put the code for "space" twice between the other codes to spread things out.)

There are four ways in which you can use paper tape. We shall discuss each one in detail.

1 SAVING PROGRAMS ON PAPER TAPE WHILE *ON-LINE*

If you have perfected a program *while using the computer on-line,* and want to save it for the future, here's what to do on the Time Share Corporation system (other systems may vary):

1. Type the word PUNCH, press the ON button on the tape punch (left side of terminal), and then press the RETURN key. The terminal will chatter away while the punch first produces a series of small holes as a lead-in (leader). Then it will punch your program into the tape (while simultaneously typing out a copy for you), and finish with a series of small holes as a trailer.

2. When the computer has finished, press the OFF button on the tape punch, and tear off the tape with a quick pull upwards. Notice the shapes of the tape ends. They are shaped like arrows pointing toward the beginning of your tape.

2 FEEDING A PROGRAM INTO THE COMPUTER FROM PAPER TAPE WHILE *ON-LINE*

1. Use your regular procedure to get your computer READY to accept BASIC programs.
2. Hold the tape with the arrows pointing toward you. Place the tape underneath the little plastic cover on the tape reader and press the small holes in the leader of the tape over the cogs in the wheel that moves the tape forward. Then close the cover.
3. On the Time Share Corporation system, you next type TAPE and press the RETURN key.
4. Push the lever on the tape reader to ON and watch the action.
5. To RUN the program now, simply type RUN. (If you wish to make changes before RUNning it, type KEY first.)

3 PREPARING A PROGRAM ON PAPER TAPE *OFF-LINE* (WITHOUT THE COMPUTER)

1. Turn the switch to LOCAL (switch on right side of terminal).
2. Press the ON button on the tape punch (left side of terminal).
3. Press the HERE IS key (upper right of terminal keyboard) to produce a "leader."

OR

Press the RUBOUT and REPT keys together (both are on right side of keyboard) until about 2 inches of tape are punched. (You should have a longer leader and trailer than those shown on page 78.)

4. Type in the statements of your program as usual *except,* at the *end* of each line, press in this order:

> the RETURN KEY
> the LINE FEED KEY

On some systems, you may also need to press:

> the RUBOUT KEY

5. If you make a typing error, you can correct it in one of two ways:
   a. Merely type a RETURN, LINE FEED, and RUBOUT, and then retype the entire line correctly;

> OR

   b. You can erase a single character by pressing the BSP (Back-SPace) button on the tape punch (left side of terminal) followed by pressing the RUBOUT key on the keyboard.
   To erase two characters, use 2 BSPs followed by 2 RUB-OUTs, and so on. After you have erased the characters, then type the correct characters and continue.
6. After finishing the program, press the HERE IS button (or press simultaneously the RUBOUT and REPT keys) to get about two inches of "trailer" tape.
7. Tear the tape off, pulling straight up.
8. Turn off the tape punch by pressing OFF and turn off the terminal (or press the CLR button).

When you're ready to try your program ON-LINE, follow the directions in 2 on page 80.

Whenever you make a tape copy of your program, be sure to write some identification on the beginning of the tape for future reference.

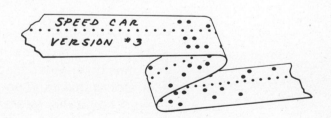

4 *OFF-LINE* DUPLICATION OF TYPEWRITTEN MATERIAL

The picture below was "drawn" on a terminal. There is no easy way to make the computer do this — in fact you shouldn't use the computer at all . . . just the terminal, *after* lots of preliminary planning at your desk. The same idea applies to "form" letters, and so on.

If you want to make such a picture, and then reproduce several copies for your friends, you should do it OFF-LINE, but with the paper tape punch turned ON. The instructions in **3** (pages 80–81) can be followed, *EXCEPT you can use only method 5b for correcting mistakes.*

When you are finished, you can then make copies, also OFF-LINE (terminal switched to LOCAL) by merely putting the tape in the paper tape reader, and pushing the lever below the tape reader to START. The same procedure can be used for duplicating listings of programs already punched on tape.

NOTE: Larger computer systems also allow you to save programs on magnetic tapes or on magnetic discs. The methods of doing this vary; so you'll have to get the information from your computer reference manual or your teacher.

3

Techniques for the Seasoned Traveler

3–1 BASIC Bulldozers

This marks the mid-point of our tour, and congratulations are in order. You can now handle input (INPUT), output (PRINT), branching (GOTO), conditional branching (IF . . . THEN), computing and storing numbers (LET), and looping (FOR-NEXT). Theoretically, just about any programming problem can be handled with this fundamental set of key words.

Of course, it's also "theoretically" true that one can move any amount of earth with a shovel, given enough ambition. However, in practice there are times when having a bulldozer available can make life much more pleasant.

This is the bulldozer part of the book — the place where advanced features of BASIC will be explained in order that complicated programming problems can be handled without backbreaking labor.

We will explain eight of these special features as follows:

FEATURE	SOME APPLICATIONS OF THE FEATURE
Variables with single subscripts	● Especially helpful in handling *lists* of values (these are called *arrays*).
REM	● A key word used to introduce descriptive comments into a program.
Variables with double subscripts	● Useful in handling values stored in *tables* (these are called *two-dimensional arrays*).
TAB	● Used for printing special output patterns.
READ — DATA	● Key words used to get lots of input into the computer.
Library Functions	● Used to do the work of many statements.
Computed GOTO	● Used to replace a group of IF . . . THEN statements.
GOSUB — RETURN	● Key words used to shorten programs that use similar groups of statements in several places.

3–2 Subscripted Variables; [DIM] and [REM]

Up to this point we have been getting along pretty well with two kinds of variable names. One is the single letter: A, B, C, . . . , Z. The other is a letter followed by a single digit: A0, A1, A2, . . . , B0, B1, B2, . . . , and so on. Let's call these "ordinary" variable names. But, as our programming gets more complicated, we'll run into trouble very soon with just "ordinary" variable names. To show this, let's use an example:

> TAKE-A-CHANCE-INTERNATIONAL AIRLINES

Suppose that TACI-Air has one flight each day of a 31-day month, and that there are three passenger seats available on each plane. We want to run a reservation office — a place where a person can request a seat for any day in the month.

Well, we can set up a board like this:

MARCH

1	2	3	4	5	6	7
A = 3	B = 3	C = 3	D = 3	E = 3	F = 3	G = 3
8	9	10	11	12	13	14
H = 3	I = 3	J = 3	K = 3	L = 3	M = 3	N = 3
15	16	17	18	19	20	21
O = 3	P = 3	Q = 3	R = 3	S = 3	T = 3	U = 3
22	23	24	25	26	27	28
V = 3	W = 3	X = 3	Y = 3	Z = 3	A1 = 3	B1 = 3
29	30	31				
C1 = 3	D1 = 3	E1 = 3				

A is the name of the variable where we store the number of seats *available* on March 1; B is for the seats available on March 2, and so on. When we start, we let A=3, B=3, and so on. If a passenger requests a ticket for March 1, we look at our board, say OK, and sell him the ticket. And then we change the value of A to 2.

Let's try automating our system so that any ticket office in the country can use a terminal to make reservations. A program to do this might start out as follows:

```
10 LET A=3
20 LET B=3
30 LET C=3
40 LET D=3
. . . . . . . . . . .
```

Hold it! Do you see that we'd need 31 LET statements just to assign the starting values for each day? That's one of the problems with "ordinary" variable names — *we* have the job of not only choosing the names but also storing values in the locations they label one at a time. Just think, if we were doing the airline reservations for the whole year, we'd need 365 separate LET statements to assign starting values!

Another trouble with "ordinary" variable names in this example is that they're not very logical; why should A stand for March 1, or P for March 16? So we need a way of naming variables where the *computer* could help choose the names and where the names would fit our situation a little better.

MARCH						
S	M	T	W	T	F	S
				1	2	3	4
5	6	7	8	9	10	11
12	13	14	15	16	17	18
19	20	21	22	23	24	25
26	27	28	29	30	(31)	

We could invent a shorthand notation calling this M(31).

Let's look at the situation a little more closely. As any calendar shows, a month is a collection of days — March is a collection of 31 days. We refer to a specific day in March by its number, for instance, March 12 or March 27.

In a similar way, we can set up a collection of computer variables. This collection is called an *array*; arrays also have names: the "M array" or "H array," for example. And (just as with months) we can talk about a specific *member* of the array by using an array name followed by a number in parentheses, for example, M(8) or H(12). These symbols are called *subscripted variables* (the number is the subscript):

M array

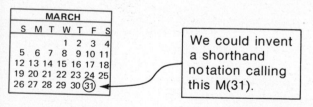

| M(1) |
| M(2) |
| M(3) |
| M(4) |
| M(5) |

Single letter ARRAY NAME   SUBSCRIPT

M(8)

M(8) is pronounced "M sub 8."

One of the best things about subscripted variables is that they help the computer keep track of where things are stored. This is because the computer "knows" that M(8) is the 8th member of the array M (just as we know that March 8 is the 8th day of March). Also, just as we know that there are 7 days of March before March 8, the computer "knows" that there are 7 members of the M array before M(8). We'll soon see how useful this is. But first let's notice:

A CRUCIAL DIFFERENCE

H8, an ordinary variable, is *not* the same as H(8), a subscripted variable. The difference is something like that between the name

HENRY EIGHT ←

> This is like an ordinary variable. "Eight" is just part of this man's name.

and the name

HENRY THE EIGHTH

> This is like a subscripted variable. The name tells us we have a whole collection of Henrys (who were Kings of England), and that *this* man is the eighth one — the eighth King of England named Henry.

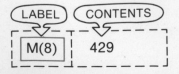

By the way, there is one similarity between ordinary and subscripted variables — both store values. That is, M(8) is a label for a memory location which can store a value (for example, 429).

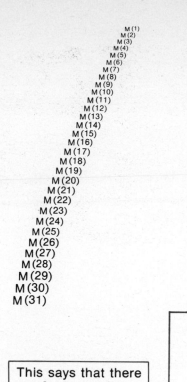

Most computers have enough storage room for arrays with quite a few members. However, it is up to us, in our programs, to indicate how many members of the array we'll need. For instance, in TACI-Air, we'll need 31 variables, one for each day of March. We warn the computer that we'll need 31 by saying

10 DIM M(31)

(Anytime you have a subscript larger than 10, you must use a DIMension statement.) After warning the computer, we can use the subscripted variables anywhere in the program.

Let's illustrate all of this by writing the complete TACI-Air program. First, let's picture a reservation board that uses subscripted variables:

MARCH

M(1) = 3	M(2) = 3	M(3) = 3	M(4) = 3	M(5) = 3	M(6) = 3	M(7) = 3
M(8) = 3	M(9) = 3	M(10) = 3	M(11) = 3	M(12) = 3	M(13) = 3	M(14) = 3

This says that there are 3 seats available on March 8.

This time we have stored the *number* of seats for the 1st day in M(1), for the 2d day in M(2), ..., for the 16th day in M(16), ..., and so on. That's logical, isn't it?

Here's how we do this in BASIC:

The warning to reserve enough space.

```
10    DIM M(31)
20    FOR D=1 TO 31
30    LET M(D)=3
40    NEXT D
```

The trick is to write

30 LET M(D)=3

and ask the computer to make D=1, 2, 3, ..., 31.

We can now assign our 31 starting values with only 4 statements! Here's the complete reservation program.

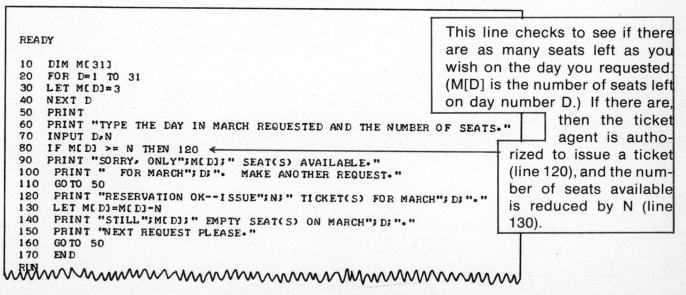

This line checks to see if there are as many seats left as you wish on the day you requested. (M[D] is the number of seats left on day number D.) If there are, then the ticket agent is authorized to issue a ticket (line 120), and the number of seats available is reduced by N (line 130).

```
READY

10    DIM M[31]
20    FOR D=1 TO 31
30    LET M[D]=3
40    NEXT D
50    PRINT
60    PRINT "TYPE THE DAY IN MARCH REQUESTED AND THE NUMBER OF SEATS."
70    INPUT D,N
80    IF M[D] >= N THEN 120
90    PRINT "SORRY, ONLY";M[D];" SEAT(S) AVAILABLE."
100   PRINT "  FOR MARCH";D;".  MAKE ANOTHER REQUEST."
110   GO TO 50
120   PRINT "RESERVATION OK--ISSUE";N;" TICKET(S) FOR MARCH";D;"."
130   LET M[D]=M[D]-N
140   PRINT "STILL";M[D];" EMPTY SEAT(S) ON MARCH";D;"."
150   PRINT "NEXT REQUEST PLEASE."
160   GO TO 50
170   END
RUN
```

A RUN is shown on the next page.

87

```
TYPE THE DAY IN MARCH REQUESTED AND THE NUMBER OF SEATS.
?5,2
RESERVATION OK--ISSUE 2 TICKET(S) FOR MARCH 5.
STILL 1 EMPTY SEAT(S) ON MARCH 5.
NEXT REQUEST PLEASE.

TYPE THE DAY IN MARCH REQUESTED AND THE NUMBER OF SEATS.
?18,1
RESERVATION OK--ISSUE 1 TICKET(S) FOR MARCH 18.
STILL 2 EMPTY SEAT(S) ON MARCH 18.
NEXT REQUEST PLEASE.

TYPE THE DAY IN MARCH REQUESTED AND THE NUMBER OF SEATS.
?5,2
SORRY, ONLY 1 SEAT(S) AVAILABLE.
   FOR MARCH 5.   MAKE ANOTHER REQUEST.

TYPE THE DAY IN MARCH REQUESTED AND THE NUMBER OF SEATS.
?6,2
RESERVATION OK--ISSUE 2 TICKET(S) FOR MARCH 6.
STILL 1 EMPTY SEAT(S) ON MARCH 6.
NEXT REQUEST PLEASE.

TYPE THE DAY IN MARCH REQUESTED AND THE NUMBER OF SEATS.
?
END
```

We decide to stop the INPUT. On Time Share Corporation installations, you press CTRL and C together, followed by RETURN.

Notice that this program does not keep a record of the reservations from one RUN to the next. A more practical program is given on page 131.

There is another interesting feature of subscripted variables that you should know about. It is OK for the subscript to be any expression, that is, a combination of variables and numbers joined by the operators $*$, $/$, $+$, $-$, and $\uparrow$.

EXAMPLES: $X(K+1)$, $X(K-1)$, $B(2*J+1)$

Exercise 1 In each row, find which variable name or names are the same as the underlined name. For example:

$\underline{G(12)}$ $\boxed{G(4*3)}$ $G(14)$ $G12$ $\boxed{G(2*6)}$ $G(12+10)$

$\underline{M9}$ $M(9)$ $M(2*4.5)$ M $M(4+5)$ $M9$ $M(16-7)$

$\underline{P(3)}$ $P(6-3)$ $P(3)$ $P3$ $P(1+2)$ $P(4-2)$ $P(27/9)$

$\underline{L(4)}$ $M(4)$ $L(16/4)$ $L4$ $L(1+1+1+1)$ $L(128/32)$

$\underline{Z(16)}$ $Z(160/10)$ $Z16$ Z $Q(16)$ $Z(256/16)$

Exercise 2 Simulate running the following program:

```
10    DIM Q(24)
20    LET M(1)=2
30    LET M(2)=8
40    LET M(3)=16
50    LET Q(4)=10
60    LET Q(6)=20
```

```
70    LET Q(24)=130
80    PRINT M(1)+M(3)
90    PRINT M(1+2)
100   PRINT M(1)+M(2)
110   PRINT Q(4*6)
120   PRINT Q(4)*Q(6)
130   PRINT Q(10+14)
140   PRINT M(28-25)
150   PRINT M(6-4)
160   PRINT Q(24/6)
170   PRINT Q(24)/Q(6)
180   PRINT M(2+1)+M(3-1)+Q(8-4)+Q(3+3)
190   END
```

Another useful statement is the REMark statement. REMark statements are placed in a program to help other people understand a *listing* of the program. REMarks are *not* printed during a RUN — only during a LIST. For example:

```
LIST


10    REM PROGRAM TO FIND AREA OF CIRCLE
20    PRINT "TYPE IN THE RADIUS (IN FEET):";
30    INPUT R
40    PRINT "AREA IS";3.14159*R*R;" SQ. FT."
50    REM THE NUMBER 3.14159 IS 'PI.'
60    END

END
RUN


TYPE IN THE RADIUS (IN FEET):?10
AREA IS 314.159 SQ. FT.
```

Exercise 3 Simulate RUNning this program:

```
10    REM PROGRAM TO PRINT SQUARES OF ANY 5 NUMBERS
20    PRINT "TYPE IN 5 NUMBERS, ONE FOR EACH '?':"
30    FOR I=1 TO 5
40    INPUT N(I)
50    NEXT I
60    PRINT "YOUR NUMBERS","SQUARES OF YOUR NUMBERS"
70    FOR K=1 TO 5
80    PRINT N(K),N(K)*N(K)
90    NEXT K
100   END
```

Exercise 4 Simulate RUNning this program:

```
10   REM PROGRAM TO GENERATE 10 FIBONACCI NUMBERS
20   LET A(1)=1
30   PRINT A(1);
40   LET A(2)=1
50   PRINT A(2);
60   FOR J=3 TO 10
70   LET A(J)=A(J-1)+A(J-2)
80   PRINT A(J);
90   NEXT J
100  END
```

NOTE: Fibonacci was a mathematician born in Pisa, Italy, in 1180. The numbers named after him are still used today in higher mathematics.

Code Name: /TRACK1/

ON-LINE

Suppose an athlete can run the 100-yard dash in 12 seconds. How fast is he going in miles per hour (mph)?

Well, 100 yards=300 feet=300/5280=.0568 mile.
And 12 seconds=12/3600=.00333 hour.
So his speed is D/T=.0568/.00333=17.0455 mph.

ON-LINE

That's a lot of arithmetic, especially if we want to do it for a list of athletes. Let's use the computer!

ON-LINE

On the next page is a program which prints the speeds for as many runners as you wish, and then gives the average speed.

After studying it and the sample RUN, see if you can modify the program so that it prints the average of only those athletes you specify. For example, you might want the average of the three highest speeds (that is, athletes 2, 4, and 5). Can you do this by letting the user INPUT the subscripts of the variables he wants averaged?

ON-LINE

```
READY

100    DIM T[20]
110    LET S=0
120    PRINT "HOW MANY TRACK 'TIMES' DO YOU WISH TO ENTER (<20)";
130    INPUT N
140    PRINT "AFTER EACH '?' ENTER A TIME (IN SECONDS) FOR THE";
150    PRINT " 100-YARD DASH."
160    FOR I=1 TO N
170    PRINT "ATHLETE #"; I;
180    INPUT T[I]
190    LET S=S+T[I]  ◄─────────────
200    NEXT I
210    PRINT
220    PRINT "HERE ARE THE TIMES AND SPEEDS:"
230    PRINT "ATHLETE #","TIME (SECONDS)","SPEED (MILES PER HOUR)"
240    FOR I=1 TO N
250    PRINT I,T[I],(300/5280)/(T[I]/3600)
260    NEXT I
270    PRINT
280    PRINT "THE AVERAGE TIME WAS"; S/N;" SECONDS."
290    PRINT "THE AVERAGE SPEED WAS";(300/5280)/((S/N)/3600);" MPH."
300    END
RUN


HOW MANY TRACK 'TIMES' DO YOU WISH TO ENTER (<20)?5
AFTER EACH '?' ENTER A TIME (IN SECONDS) FOR THE 100-YARD DASH.
ATHLETE # 1?15.3
ATHLETE # 2?12.0
ATHLETE # 3?14.1
ATHLETE # 4?11.3
ATHLETE # 5?9.8

HERE ARE THE TIMES AND SPEEDS:
ATHLETE #       TIME (SECONDS) SPEED (MILES PER HOUR)
   1               15.3          13.369
   2               12            17.0455
   3               14.1          14.5068
   4               11.3          18.1014
   5               9.8           20.872

THE AVERAGE TIME WAS 12.5 SECONDS.
THE AVERAGE SPEED WAS 16.3636 MPH.
```

> S is used to find the SUM of all the "times." The average time will then be S/N.

Code Name: /AIRLINE1/

Run the TACI-Airline reservation program for several customers.

Code Name: /AIRLINE2/

Add the following statements to your airline program and see what happens (type 0, 0 as the last INPUT):

```
75   IF D=0 THEN 162
162  PRINT
164  PRINT "SEATS LEFT FOR THE MONTH OF MARCH ARE (DAY, SEATS):"
165  FOR D=1 TO 31
166  PRINT D;M(D);"    ";
168  NEXT D
```

Here's a good example of the value of subscripts. This program *sorts* a collection of numbers into ascending (increasing) order. After studying the program and running it, see if you can write a similar program to put numbers into descending (decreasing) order.

```
READY

100    PRINT "PROGRAM TO SORT A LIST OF NUMBERS INTO ASCENDING ORDER"
110    DIM L[100]
120    PRINT
130    PRINT "HOW MANY NUMBERS ARE TO BE SORTED";
140    INPUT N
150    PRINT "TYPE IN THE LIST OF NUMBERS ONE AT A TIME:"
160    FOR I=1 TO N
170    INPUT L[I]
180    NEXT I
190    FOR K=1 TO N-1
200    FOR J=1 TO N-K
210    IF L[J] <= L[J+1] THEN 250
220    LET T=L[J]
230    LET L[J]=L[J+1]
240    LET L[J+1]=T
250    NEXT J
260    NEXT K
270    PRINT
280    PRINT "THE SORTED LIST IS:"
290    FOR I=1 TO N
300    PRINT L[I],
310    NEXT I
320    END
RUN


PROGRAM TO SORT A LIST OF NUMBERS INTO ASCENDING ORDER

HOW MANY NUMBERS ARE TO BE SORTED?5
TYPE IN THE LIST OF NUMBERS ONE AT A TIME:
?3.25
?4.68
?98.32
?0.78
?12.5

THE SORTED LIST IS:
 .78            3.25           4.68           12.5           98.32
```

> This is the tricky part. It swaps the number in L(J) with the number in L(J+1).

Challenge Combine the //SORT// program with the program /TRACK1/ to put the athletes' records in the order of first place, second place, and so on, and then to give the average time for the first three places.

3–3 Two-dimensional Arrays

A new mayor of Ashbank has just been elected. One of his main campaign promises was to make Ashbank a safe place in which to live.

His first directive is to the police department — cut down the number of traffic accidents. So the police commissioner's first move is an order to his computing division — get statistics on the number of accidents at each intersection.

Let's look at a map of downtown Ashbank and help ABC (The Ashbank Bureau of Computing) analyze the problem:

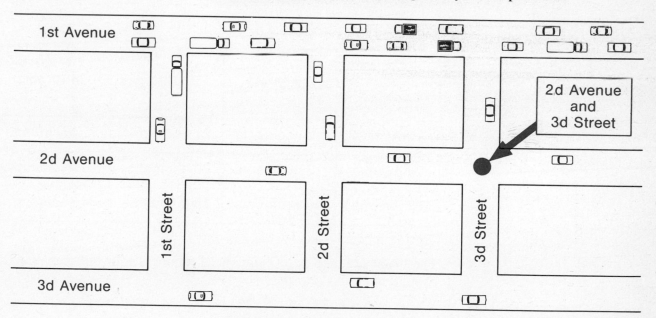

First, we'll need an easy way to refer to a particular intersection.

Second, we'll have to be able to associate the number of accidents at the intersection with the name of the intersection.

We could letter the intersections with single letters, or we could use subscripted variables. Which shall it be? Well, the downtown area is rapidly expanding — so our method should make it easy to add other intersections in the future. Also, the streets already have numbers — why not use them?

With these facts in mind, we could refer to the intersections by first giving the AVENUE name, and then giving the intersecting STREET name. The intersection in our picture marked with a heavy dot is "2d AVE and 3d ST."

This suggests that it would be nice to have a second type of subscripted variable, one that has *two* subscripts. Here's what these variables look like in BASIC:

> $N(2,3)$ represents the number of accidents at 2d AVE and 3d ST. $N(1,2)$ represents the number of accidents at 1st AVE and 2d ST and so on.

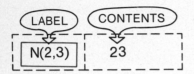

Just as with single-subscript variables, the double-subscript variables store values. So if, in the past year, 23 accidents have taken place at 2d AVE and 3d ST, we can say:

>   LET N(2,3)=23

If 21 occurred at 1st AVE and 2d ST, we can say:

>   LET N(1,2)=21

We can think of these storage locations as if they were arranged in a table. The *contents* are the numbers of accidents at each intersection.

Street / Avenue	1st Street	2d Street	3d Street
1st Avenue	46 accidents	21 accidents	72 accidents
2d Avenue	13 accidents	28 accidents	23 accidents
3d Avenue	16 accidents	18 accidents	34 accidents

The usual practice is to enter these numbers into the computer by rows, that is, in the order:

>   46, 21, 72, 13, 28, 23, 16, 18, 34

The best way to compare the safety of the different intersections is to find each intersection's percentage of the total accidents in Ashbank. If we found, for instance, that one intersection has 37%, and another has 21%, then it would be clear that the former for some reason is much more dangerous.

So we write the program shown on the next page.

```
READY
10    PRINT "TYPE IN THE NUMBER OF ACCIDENTS AT EACH INTERSECTION"
20    PRINT "IN THE ORDER 1ST AVENUE AND 1ST STREET, 1ST AVENUE AND"
30    PRINT "2D STREET, AND SO ON."
40    LET T=0
50    FOR A=1 TO 3
60    FOR S=1 TO 3
70    INPUT N[A,S]
80    LET T=T+N[A,S]
90    NEXT S
100   NEXT A
110   PRINT
120   PRINT " AVE    AND    STREET","% OF TOTAL"
130   FOR A=1 TO 3
140   FOR S=1 TO 3
150   PRINT A;" AVE AND";S;" ST ",(N[A,S]/T)*100;"%"
160   NEXT S
170   NEXT A
180   PRINT
190   PRINT "1ST AVE'S PERCENTAGE IS";(N[1,1]+N[1,2]+N[1,3])/T*100;"%."
200   PRINT "2D AVE'S PERCENTAGE IS";(N[2,1]+N[2,2]+N[2,3])/T*100;"%."
210   PRINT "3D AVE'S PERCENTAGE IS";(N[3,1]+N[3,2]+N[3,3])/T*100;"%."
220   END
RUN

TYPE IN THE NUMBER OF ACCIDENTS AT EACH INTERSECTION
IN THE ORDER 1ST AVENUE AND 1ST STREET, 1ST AVENUE AND
2D STREET, AND SO ON.
?46
?21
?72
?13
?28
?23
?16
?18
?34

AVE    AND    STREET         % OF TOTAL
1 AVE AND 1 ST              16.9742%
1 AVE AND 2 ST              7.74908%
1 AVE AND 3 ST             26.5683%
2 AVE AND 1 ST              4.79705%
2 AVE AND 2 ST             10.3321%
2 AVE AND 3 ST              8.48709%
3 AVE AND 1 ST              5.90406%
3 AVE AND 2 ST              6.64207%
3 AVE AND 3 ST             12.5461%

1ST AVE'S PERCENTAGE IS 51.2915%.
2D AVE'S PERCENTAGE IS 23.6162%.
3D AVE'S PERCENTAGE IS 25.0923%.
```

You can see that 1st Avenue clearly has the most accidents — over 50% of all the accidents in Ashbank. There should no longer be any doubt that 1st Avenue needs some traffic lights.

The most complex parts of the program are the nested FOR loops in lines 50–100 and 130–170.

Let's make a table to see how the nested FOR loops work.

FOR A→1   Ⓐ Ⓢ

    FOR S→1 $N(1,1)$ 1st AVE and 1st ST
        →2 $N(1,2)$ 1st AVE and 2d ST
        →3 $N(1,3)$ 1st AVE and 3d ST

FOR A→2

    FOR S→1 $N(2,1)$ 2d AVE and 1st ST
        →2 $N(2,2)$ 2d AVE and 2d ST
        →3 $N(2,3)$ 2d AVE and 3d ST

FOR A→3

    FOR S→1 $N(3,1)$ 3d AVE and 1st ST
        →2 $N(3,2)$ 3d AVE and 2d ST
        →3 $N(3,3)$ 3d AVE and 3d ST

Line 80 finds the total number of accidents in Ashbank.

Line 150 prints the percentage of all accidents happening at each *intersection*.

And lines 190–210 find the percentages of accidents by *avenues*.

Code Name: /ACCIDENT/

Change and RUN the above program for a town that has 16 dangerous intersections (4 streets and 4 avenues).

	1st Street	2d Street	3d Street	4th Street
1st Avenue	3 accidents	8 accidents	6 accidents	2 accidents
2d Avenue	2 accidents	14 accidents	11 accidents	9 accidents
3d Avenue	2 accidents	4 accidents	5 accidents	3 accidents
4th Avenue	1 accident	3 accidents	2 accidents	0 accidents

Just as with single-subscript variables, the double-subscript variables must have DIMension statements if subscripts greater than 10 are to be used. Suppose, for example, you wanted to run /ACCIDENT/ for a town with 15 avenues and 20 streets. Then you would need to add the statement:

    1 DIM N(15,20)

WARNING: Since this requires 300 memory locations, it might not work on some minicomputers.

3–4 Using TAB in PRINT Statements

If you're bored with numbers, PRINT TAB is the answer! PRINT TAB allows you to make graphs, draw designs, plot curves, and, generally, to have fun.

Here's how it works: You have to tell the computer two main things:

● What to print, and
● Where to print it.

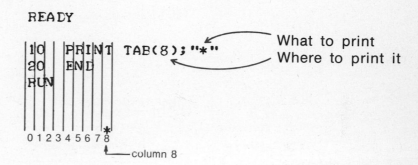

The 8 is the number of a space on the terminal paper. The terminal paper is thought of as having 72 spaces, or *columns,* numbered from 0 to 71.

Statement 10 above tells the computer to go to column 8 and print an asterisk (∗) there. The statement

10 PRINT TAB(14);"∗"; TAB(20);"∗"

would print two asterisks, one in column 14 and one in column 20.

That's the general idea; now for some specifics:

1 You can print anything at the specified position: Nonnumeric characters must be placed within quotation marks; numbers do not need quotation marks.

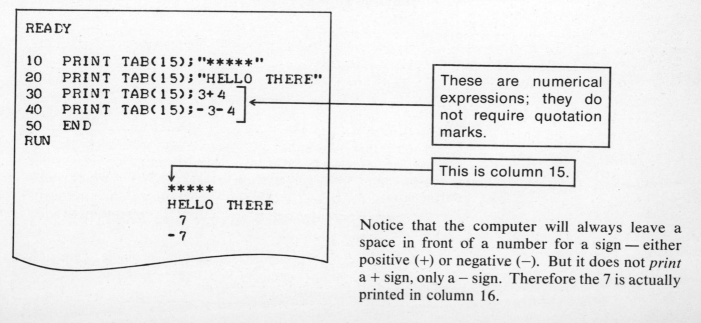

Notice that the computer will always leave a space in front of a number for a sign — either positive (+) or negative (−). But it does not *print* a + sign, only a − sign. Therefore the 7 is actually printed in column 16.

2. A variable can be used to tell the computer where to print:
If X equals 10,

```
PRINT TAB(X);"*"
```

means the same as:

```
PRINT TAB(10);"*"
```

If M equals 64,

```
PRINT TAB(M);"*"
```

means the same as:

```
PRINT TAB(64);"*"
```

You can also specify several columns in which the computer is to print. (See the next example.)

3. Once the carriage is in a position, it cannot move backwards (the terminal has no backspace); only TABs to further positions along a line will be carried out. For instance:

```
READY

10   PRINT TAB(5);"*";TAB(10);"+";TAB(15);"-"
20   END
RUN


     *    +    -
```

Column   5   10   15

If you use a decimal number with TAB, only the whole number part is used:

PRINT TAB(19.788) is taken to mean PRINT TAB(19)

To show you what's going on, let's use an example. One simple design for the computer to print is a tree. On the next page is a LISTing of the tree program and a RUN.

The first FOR loop will cause the computer to print 10 pairs of asterisks. The positions of the two asterisks in each row are:

I	TAB(35−I)	TAB(35+I)
1	34	36
2	33	37
3	32	38
4	31	39
5	30	40
.	.	.
.	.	.
.	.	.
10	25	45

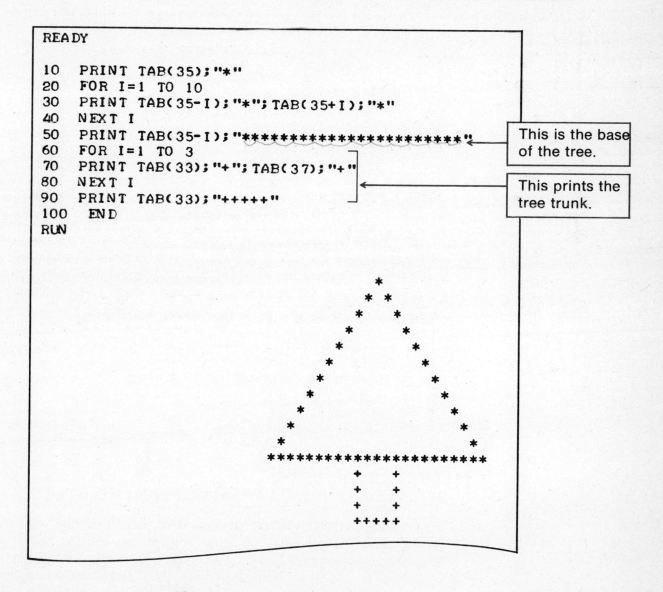

```
READY

10    PRINT TAB(35); "*"
20    FOR I=1 TO 10
30    PRINT TAB(35-I); "*"; TAB(35+I); "*"
40    NEXT I
50    PRINT TAB(35-I); "************************"      ← This is the base of the tree.
60    FOR I=1 TO 3
70    PRINT TAB(33); "+"; TAB(37); "+"                ← This prints the tree trunk.
80    NEXT I
90    PRINT TAB(33); "+++++"
100   END
RUN
```

Code Name: /TREE/

Modify the above program to print a tree that is about twice as tall as the one shown.

ON-LINE

Code Name: //BRAKE//

Write a program that makes a "graph" of the distance it takes a car to stop if it is going 10, 15, 20, . . . , 80 miles per hour. Use the formula:

Distance needed to stop (in "car lengths")=.01*S*S (S=speed in MPH) or in BASIC:

LET D=.01*S*S

Here's a sample output:

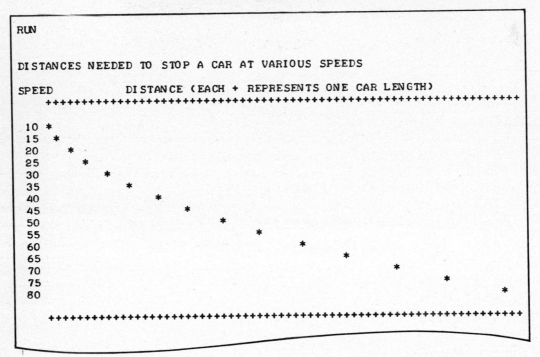

```
RUN

DISTANCES NEEDED TO STOP A CAR AT VARIOUS SPEEDS

SPEED            DISTANCE (EACH + REPRESENTS ONE CAR LENGTH)
     ++++++++++++++++++++++++++++++++++++++++++++++++++++++++++++
  10 *
  15  *
  20   *
  25    *
  30     *
  35      *
  40       *
  45        *
  50         *
  55          *
  60           *
  65            *
  70             *
  75              *
  80               *

     ++++++++++++++++++++++++++++++++++++++++++++++++++++++++++++
```

If you need some help, first try this simple program:

```
 5 LET S=40
10 LET D=S*S*.01
20 PRINT S;TAB(D+3);"*"
30 END
```

3–5 READ and DATA Statements; RESTORE

We've discussed the INPUT statement (page 37) as one way of getting *data* (values) into a program. When you use the INPUT statement, the computer types a ? and then waits for you to type in a value. After you type it in and press RETURN, the computer then uses that number in its calculations. But, if you have a lot of data which won't change from RUN to RUN, there is a better method for getting information into the computer. This method uses the READ and DATA statements.

Look at the program at the left below.

How did that work? The keyword READ tells the computer that some variables follow which don't have any values as yet. To find their values, the computer searches for a DATA statement where the values are listed.

So, in our example, at line 10, the computer "sees" the keyword READ, and then the A; it searches for a DATA statement, finds it, and then stores the first value in the DATA statement in location A.

```
10 READ A, . . .
20
30
40 DATA ② . . .
```

Values for B and C and D are found in the same way.

```
10 READ A,B,C,D
20
30
40 DATA ② ③ ④ ⑩
```

When finished with line 10, the computer has given A the value 2, B the value 3, C the value 4, and D the value 10. At line 20, using A, B, C and D, the value of X is calculated (X=2*3*4+10=34).

Look at this program:

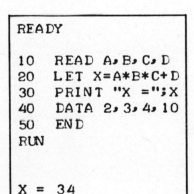

```
READY

10    READ A, B, C, D
20    LET X=A*B*C+D
30    PRINT "X =";X
40    DATA 2, 3, 4, 10
50    END
RUN


X = 34
```

```
READY

10    READ F, G, H, M
20    PRINT F+G+H+M
30    DATA 23, 32, 10, 1
40    END
RUN


66
```

F equals	23
G equals	32
H equals	10
M equals	1
	66

There are several interesting variations possible with READ-DATA statements:

1. We can have more than one READ statement for one DATA statement. The various READ statements use the values in the DATA statement one by one. When a value has been used, it cannot be used again (unless you do something special as explained on page 104). For example:

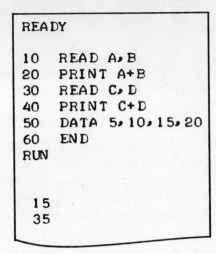

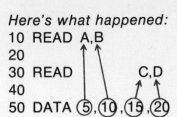

Here's what happened:

2. We can also have several DATA statements. It does not matter to the computer where the DATA statements are located in the program, or how many DATA statements are used. The computer combines all of the DATA statements into one big list of values, which will be used one by one by the READ statements. So

        50 DATA 2,3,4,5

is the same as:

        50 DATA 2
        51 DATA 3,4
        52 DATA 5

Query Is

        50 DATA 2
        51 DATA 4,3
        52 DATA 5

the same as the first two examples?

Answer No, since the numbers are not in the same *order* as in the original DATA list.

Here's another example of several READ and DATA statements in one program:

```
READY

10    READ A,B
20    PRINT A+B
30    READ C,D,E
40    DATA 5
50    PRINT A+C+E-D
60    DATA 10
70    DATA 15,20
80    DATA 25
90    END
RUN

  15
  25
```

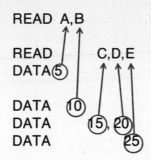

3. Two other possibilities can occur:
   a. One is that there are fewer variables in the READ statements than values in the DATA statements. In this case, only the values in the DATA statement needed by the READ statements are used.

```
READY

10    READ A,B
20    PRINT B-A
30    READ C,D,E
40    PRINT C*D*E+B-A
50    DATA 1,4,5,20,10,97,33
60    END
RUN

   3
 1003
```

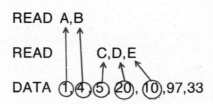

The 97 and 33 are never used.

   b. On the other hand, there may be fewer values in the DATA statements than variables in the READ statements. If the computer finds that it needs more values than are provided, it halts the RUNning of the program, and types a message that says: "OUT OF DATA." For example:

```
READY

10    READ A,B
20    READ C
30    PRINT A+B+C
40    DATA 5,10
50    END
RUN




OUT OF DATA   IN LINE 20
```

READ A,B
READ ↑ ↑ C
DATA ⑤ ⑩ ⟨⟩

The moral is that the *programmer* must make sure that variables and data match, if that's what he wants.

4. It is possible to use the same data over and over by using the RESTORE statement. The RESTORE statement is particularly useful when the same data is to be used at several places in the program. Here's an example:

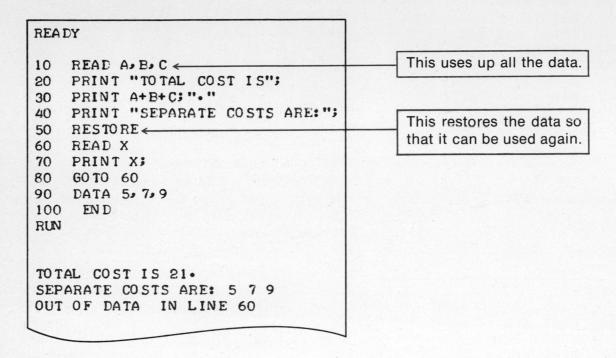

```
READY

10    READ A, B, C          ←──────  This uses up all the data.
20    PRINT "TOTAL COST IS";
30    PRINT A+B+C; "."
40    PRINT "SEPARATE COSTS ARE:";
50    RESTORE  ←──────────────────  This restores the data so
60    READ X                        that it can be used again.
70    PRINT X;
80    GOTO 60
90    DATA 5, 7, 9
100   END
RUN


TOTAL COST IS 21.
SEPARATE COSTS ARE: 5 7 9
OUT OF DATA  IN LINE 60
```

A QUICK SUMMARY:

● For giving many variables values, READ-DATA statements are much more efficient than INPUT or LET statements, especially if the program is to be RUN several times.

● The READ statement names the variables in which the values are to be stored.

● The DATA statement contains the values which will be stored in the variables.

● It's the programmer's responsibility to make sure that the variables in the READ statement match the values in the DATA statement.

EXERCISES

Simulate running each of these programs.

```
10    LET A=12
20    PRINT A
30    READ A,B
40    PRINT A*B
50    DATA 8,10
60    END
```

```
10    FOR I=1 TO 5
20    READ A,B
30    PRINT I;A;B
40    NEXT I
50    DATA 2,4,4,8,6,12,8,16,10,20
60    END
```

```
10    READ A,B,C,D
20    PRINT A*B
30    PRINT D/C
40    PRINT B+C
50    DATA 2,24,12,36
60    END
```

```
10    READ M,T,F,W
20    PRINT M+W
30    PRINT W*M
40    IF T/F>10 THEN 60
50    STOP
60    PRINT W+M
70    DATA 1,15
80    DATA 3,1
90    END
```

```
10    DATA 5,10,15
20    READ R,S
30    PRINT R+S
40    READ T
50    RESTORE
60    READ U,V,W
70    IF T=U THEN 100
80    IF S=V THEN 110
90    GOTO 120
100   PRINT "YOU'RE WRONG"
105   GOTO 120
110   PRINT "YOU'RE RIGHT"
120   END
```

Code Name: /WEATHER1/

When the United States Weather Bureau (now the National Weather Service) was established in 1870, records of weather patterns were kept for the first time. Temperature patterns were in part determined by comparing average monthly temperatures from year to year. At the Marquette, Michigan, station, the average monthly temperatures for 1874 and 1875 were as given in the table below.

Using READ-DATA statements, write a program which finds the difference between temperatures in 1874 and 1875 for each month.

Month / Year	JAN 1	FEB 2	MAR 3	APR 4	MAY 5	JUNE 6	JULY 7	AUG 8	SEPT 9	OCT 10	NOV 11	DEC 12
1874	19.0°	18.9°	23.3°	29.6°	51.3°	58.1°	65.3°	64.4°	60.0°	45.7°	29.9°	21.0°
1875	5.9°	1.3°	19.4°	33.3°	48.5°	56.7°	63.0°	61.5°	52.8°	39.9°	28.5°	25.7°

Hint: Arrange the DATA statements like this:

```
100  DATA  19.0,18.9,23.3,29.6,51.3,58.1,65.3,64.4,60.0,45.7,29.9,21.0
110  DATA  5.9,1.3,19.4,33.3,48.5,56.7,63.0,61.5,52.8,39.9,28.5,25.7
```

Then READ the DATA for each year (FOR I=1 TO 12, READ A(I), NEXT I — for the months in 1874; FOR I=1 TO 12, READ B(I), NEXT I — for the data from 1875). In a loop, find the difference between each A(I) and B(I) and print it out. A part of a RUN might look like this:

```
MONTH    1874    1875    DIFFERENCE (DEGREES)
  1      19.0    5.9           −13.1
  2      18.9    1.3           −17.6
  3      23.3    19.4          −3.9
..........................................
```

Code Name: /WEATHER2/

Change your program so that if the month in 1875 is warmer than its respective month in 1874, the program prints out:

MONTH (number) IS WARMER BY ? DEGREES.

If it's colder, print out:

MONTH (number) IS COLDER BY ? DEGREES.

Code Name: ///SURVEY///

Write a program that tabulates opinions taken from a questionnaire of the following type (or invent questions of your own choice):

Name: _____ Age:____ Male ☐ Female ☐

1 The President should wear a beard:
      1=Agree
      2=Disagree
      3=No opinion

2 April 15 should be a holiday:
      1=Agree
      2=Disagree
      3=No opinion

3 Schools should remain open all summer:
      1=Agree
      2=Disagree
      3=No Opinion

Your program should use a separate DATA statement for each person who fills out a questionnaire. The numbers in each DATA statement should mean the following (use 1 for male, 0 for female):

Opinion on Question

(Sex) (Age)   #1   #2   #3

First Questionnaire→901 DATA 0, 18, 2, 1, 2
Second Questionnaire→902 DATA 1, 16, 2, 3, 1
Third Questionnaire→903 . . . .

A RUN of your program should look like this:

```
RUN


DATA GATHERED ON QUESTIONNAIRE

                            AGREED      DISAGREED    NO OPINION
   1    FEMALE VOTE:        1           4            5
        MALE VOTE:          4           1            5
        UNDER AGE 16 VOTE:  3           1            3
   2    FEMALE VOTE:        1           4            5
        MALE VOTE:          1           7            2
        UNDER AGE 16 VOTE:  1           4            2
   3    FEMALE VOTE:        3           1            6
        MALE VOTE:          3           5            2
        UNDER AGE 16 VOTE:  2           2            3
```

Here's *part* of the program that produced this RUN:

```
130    READ N
140    FOR I=1 TO 3
150    FOR J=1 TO 3
160    LET X[I,J]=0
170    LET Y[I,J]=0
180    LET Z[I,J]=0
190    NEXT J
200    NEXT I
210    FOR I=1 TO N
220    READ S,A
230    FOR J=1 TO 3
240    READ C
250    IF S=1 THEN 280
260    LET X[J,C]=X[J,C]+1
270    GO TO 290
280    LET Y[J,C]=Y[J,C]+1
290    IF A >= 16 THEN 310
300    LET Z[J,C]=Z[J,C]+1
310    NEXT J
320    NEXT I
330    FOR I=1 TO 3
340    PRINT I; TAB(5); "FEMALE VOTE:"TAB(30); X[I,1];
350    PRINT TAB(40); X[I,2]; TAB(53); X[I,3]

700    DATA 20
710    DATA 0,15,1,1,1
720    DATA 0,33,2,3,3
730    DATA 1,21,1,3,2
740    DATA 0,22,2,2,3
750    DATA 1,36,3,2,1
760    DATA 1,14,3,2,3
770    DATA 0,13,3,3,3
780    DATA 0,55,3,3,1
790    DATA 1,49,1,3,2
800    DATA 1,32,3,1,1
810    DATA 0,44,2,2,2
820    DATA 1,56,3,2,2
830    DATA 0,32,2,2,3
```

Extra: Modify your program so that it prints the *percentage* of people who voted in each category.

3–6 Some "Library" Functions in BASIC: SQR , INT , ABS , RND

Like most things in computer programming, functions are easier to use than explain. However, it will help if we take the time to introduce some new terminology — words like *function*, *argument*, and *value*. This will make it possible to give an accurate description of exactly what happens when you use functions in a program.

Functions are actually small programs stored inside the computer. There are quite a few of these available in BASIC, and the *collection* of functions that you can call upon is often called a *library* of functions. In this section we'll discuss four of the library functions found in every version of BASIC.

SQR Here are two BASIC programs that use the SQR (square root) function:

```
READY

10 LET X=SQR(25)
20 PRINT X
30 END
RUN


 5
```

OR

```
READY

10 PRINT SQR(25)
20 END
RUN


 5
```

SQR is a function which gives you the square root of a number. You supply a number which is called the ARGUMENT. SQR then returns the VALUE of the function — which is the square root of the number. So we have:

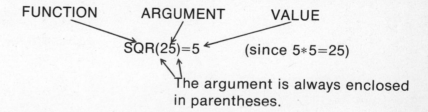

FUNCTION   ARGUMENT   VALUE

SQR(25)=5   (since 5∗5=25)

The argument is always enclosed in parentheses.

In general, a function can be used at any place in a program where a variable is used; *except* — you can never use a function on the *left* side of a LET statement (because a function is not a location in which you can store a value).

Here's a program that uses the SQR function in two statements:

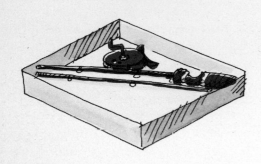

Problem How long can sections of a fishing rod be to fit into a flat rectangular box?

Answer From geometry we know that the "diagonal" of such a box is given by:

DIAGONAL=SQUARE ROOT OF (L×L+W×W)

In BASIC we would say:

LET D=SQR(L*L+W*W)

Here's a program which uses this formula, with the lengths in inches:

```
READY

10   PRINT "TYPE LENGTH OF BOX, WIDTH OF BOX, AND LENGTH OF SECTION:"
20   INPUT L,W,R
30   LET D=SQR(L*L+W*W)
40   IF D<R THEN 70
50   PRINT "THE FISHING ROD WILL FIT."
60   STOP
70   PRINT "THE FISHING ROD WON'T FIT."
80   PRINT "THE DIAGONAL OF THE BOX IS ONLY";
90   PRINT D;" INCHES."
100   END
RUN


TYPE LENGTH OF BOX, WIDTH OF BOX, AND LENGTH OF SECTION:
?20,15,28
THE FISHING ROD WON'T FIT.
THE DIAGONAL OF THE BOX IS ONLY 25 INCHES.
```

Notice in statements 30 and 80 that the *argument* of the SQR function is allowed to be an expression.

When using functions, you should be aware of the *order* in which the computer does things. Operations within the argument of the function are done first, then the function is evaluated, and, finally, all other arithmetic operations in the statement are done in the usual order (see page 23).

```
READY

10    LET F=36
20    PRINT SQR(F)
30    PRINT SQR(4*F)
40    PRINT SQR(F-11)+10
50    PRINT 2*SQR(SQR(4*F)*3)



60    PRINT SQR(-36)
70    END
RUN


   6
  12
  15
  12

SQR OF NEGATIVE ARGUMENT IN LINE 60
```

Function	Argument	Value	Printed
SQR	F=36	6	6
SQR	4*F=144	12	12
SQR	F-11=25	5	15
SQR ①	4*F=144	12	
SQR ②	12*3=36	6	12
SQR	-36		Error message

A negative argument is not accepted. We cannot take the square root of a negative number.

Code Name: /PIZZA/

Let's suppose you are a very neat eater, and only take 1-square-inch bites when consuming a pizza.

Question How many such bites are in a 10″ diameter pizza?

Answer $A=\pi \times r \times r=78.5397$ sq.-in. bites as found in the program below.

Your problem is to improve the given program so that you can also input the price of the pizza. The program should then tell you both the number of square-inch bites and the *cost* per bite. Use your program to find out which is the best buy: 8″ pizza @ $0.75, or 10″ pizza @ $1.00, or 12″ pizza @ $1.50.

ON-LINE ON-LINE ON-LINE ON-LINE ON-LINE ON-LINE

```
READY

10    INPUT D
20    LET R=D/2
30    LET A=3.14159*R*R
40    PRINT "THERE ARE";A;" SQUARE-INCH BITES IN A(N)";D;"-INCH PIZZA."
50    END
RUN


?10
THERE ARE 78.5397 SQUARE-INCH BITES IN A(N) 10-INCH PIZZA.
```

Code Name: //INVERSE PIZZA//

Now let's look at the reverse problem: How big a pizza (diameter) do you need to feed a crowd of P people if each person is to get a given number (call it B) of 1-square-inch bites?

Some information you'll need:

● The radius of a pizza with A square inches of eating is given by

LET R=SQR(A/3.14159)

● Pizzas are ordered by their diameter D, and D=2*R.

Write a program that allows you to input the number of people coming to your pizza party, and the number of 1-square-inch bites each person is to get.

The output should be like the following:

```
RUN

HOW MANY PEOPLE AT YOUR PARTY? 10
HOW MANY SQUARE-INCH BITES EACH? 31
IF YOU ORDER 1 PIZZA(S), THE DIAMETER(S) SHOULD BE AT LEAST 19.8672
INCHES.
IF YOU ORDER 2 PIZZA(S), THE DIAMETER(S) SHOULD BE AT LEAST 14.0482
INCHES.
IF YOU ORDER 3 PIZZA(S), THE DIAMETER(S) SHOULD BE AT LEAST 11.4703
INCHES.
```

Output should continue until the diameter goes below 8 inches.

INT Another function in the BASIC library is one that takes the *integer* part of the argument. INT(N) is defined on most computers as the greatest integer less than or equal to N. If N is not an integer, then INT(N) is the closest integer to the *left* of N, pictured on the usual horizontal number line. If you look at the picture below, you'll see that

INT(2.3)=2
INT(.8)=0

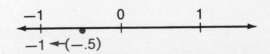

If N is an integer, then INT(N)=N.

Question: What does INT(−.5) mean? Here's the way our rule works:

a. If the argument is positive, then the largest whole number "to the left" can be found by chopping off the decimal part (therefore, INT(2.3)=2).

b. If the argument is negative, then the largest whole number contained in the argument is still the integer "to the left" of the argument. Therefore INT (−.5)=−1.

Now let's look at a few uses of the INT function.

To find out if a whole number is even or odd, we can use the INT function very nicely:

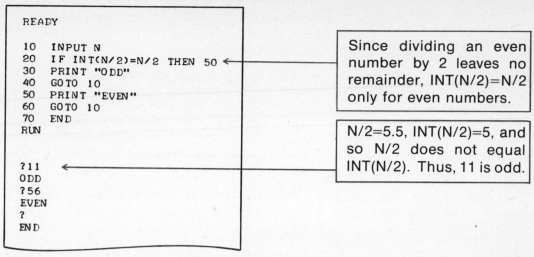

```
READY

10   INPUT N
20   IF INT(N/2)=N/2 THEN 50
30   PRINT "ODD"
40   GOTO 10
50   PRINT "EVEN"
60   GOTO 10
70   END
RUN


?11
ODD
?56
EVEN
?
END
```

Since dividing an even number by 2 leaves no remainder, INT(N/2)=N/2 only for even numbers.

N/2=5.5, INT(N/2)=5, and so N/2 does not equal INT(N/2). Thus, 11 is odd.

The INT function is very commonly used in another way. Let's say we had $10.00 and wanted to divide it equally among three people. Let's see how much each person gets. The program at the left gives the answer.

```
READY

10   LET A=10/3
20   PRINT "$";A
30   END
RUN


$ 3.33333
```

But money is only expressed with two decimal places — we'd like $3.33, instead of $3.33333. How do we chop off the extra 3's?

We want 2 digits after the decimal point; so we multiply by 100, take the INT part, and then divide by 100.

$$INT(100*3.33333)/100$$
$$=INT(333.333)/100$$
$$=333/100$$

But, 333/100=3.33, which is what we wanted. (This program doesn't say who gets the extra penny.)

How would we have got one decimal place? We would have multiplied by 10, taken the integer part, and then divided by 10:

$$INT(10*3.33333)/10$$
$$=INT(33.3333)/10$$
$$=33/10$$
$$=3.3$$

In general, if you want a number to have N decimal places (and it has more than N places), use the following:

$$INT((10\uparrow N)*\text{old number})/(10\uparrow N)$$

If you want the value rounded, use

$$INT((10\uparrow N*\text{old number}+.5)/(10\uparrow N)$$

ABS ABS is a BASIC function which returns the ABSOLUTE VALUE of a number. The function is written ABS (X).

$$ABS(10)=10$$
$$ABS(0)=0$$
$$ABS(-10)=10$$
$$ABS(-427)=427$$

Notice that ABS(15−10)=5 and ABS(10−15)=5.

Try this program to see why that's useful:

Code Name: /ELEVATOR/

```
READY

5   PRINT "THIS PROGRAM ASSUMES A BUILDING WITH 15 FEET BETWEEN FLOORS."
10  PRINT "WHAT FLOOR IS THE ELEVATOR ON";
20  INPUT A
30  PRINT "TO WHICH FLOOR IS IT GOING";
40  INPUT B
50  PRINT "THE NUMBER OF FEET THE ELEVATOR TRAVELS IS";
60  PRINT 15*ABS(A-B);"."
70  END
RUN


THIS PROGRAM ASSUMES A BUILDING WITH 15 FEET BETWEEN FLOORS.
WHAT FLOOR IS THE ELEVATOR ON?8
TO WHICH FLOOR IS IT GOING?18
THE NUMBER OF FEET THE ELEVATOR TRAVELS IS 150.

END
```

RND The last function which we will discuss is the random number function RND. RND causes the computer to select a "surprise" number between 0 (zero) and 1; in other words a number like .032145, .285467, or .765321.

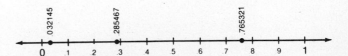

It's as though the computer spun a wheel of chance, like the one in our picture, to get the *value* for the RND function; we're never quite sure what number will be selected.

Sorry to have to say this again, but this function varies slightly among computers, and the best way to find out about it is to check your computer manual, ask your teacher, or (best of all) experiment. Here are some suggestions.

The general form of the function is RND(X). On some computers, the value of X is not important; on other computers, it makes a difference. You'll see how this works on the next page. But first you should try an experiment. RUN the following program *twice:*

```
READY

10    FOR K=1 TO 5
20    PRINT RND(1),
30    NEXT K
40    END
RUN
```

Here's the result of the preceding experiment on two different computer systems which we'll call A and B.

Computer A

```
RUN

 .731631      .893412      .660973      .685044      .655552

END
RUN

 .619889      .728673      .222167      9.70735E-02  .766305

END
```

Computer B

```
RUN

 .529432      .225555      .329078      .306689      .537845

END
RUN

 .529432      .225555      .329078      .306689      .537845

END
```

Computer A produced a completely *different* set of random numbers on each RUN. For the applications in this book, this is preferred. If your computer acted like computer A, you're all set!

If your computer acted like computer B, there are three things you can try doing to make it act like computer A, producing a real "surprise" on every RUN.

1. On some systems, you add a statement containing RND(−1) at the beginning of the program. RUN this program twice.

```
READY

5   LET X=RND(-1)
10   FOR K=1 TO 5
20   PRINT RND(1),
30   NEXT K
40   END
RUN
```

2. On other systems, the way to get different random numbers on every RUN is to change statement 5 to read:

5 RANDOMIZE

The rest of the program stays the same.

3. If none of the above work, there is a somewhat clumsy way of making each RUN be "almost" a surprise. It takes five extra statements as follows:

```
READY

5   PRINT "TYPE THE SECOND HAND'S POSITION ON WALL CLOCK";
6   INPUT S
7   FOR J=1 TO S
8   LET X=RND(1)
9   NEXT J
10   FOR K=1 TO 5
20   PRINT RND(1),
30   NEXT K
40   END
RUN


TYPE THE SECOND HAND'S POSITION ON WALL CLOCK?26
 .38255        .598038        .995577        .168938        .953169


END
RUN


TYPE THE SECOND HAND'S POSITION ON WALL CLOCK?45
 .366534       .34335         .61215         .748658        .512073


END
```

The user typed in 26 after the first RUN to indicate that the second hand on a clock "happened" to show 26 seconds past the minute. Lines 7, 8, and 9 then forced the computer to run down its list of random numbers to the 26th one before printing anything in line 20. On the second RUN, since the clock happened to show 45 seconds, a different number in the list was used as the starting point.

One last thing — if your computer acts like A, and you *want* it to act like B, try experiment ☐1. This technique works in reverse on some computers!

Now let's look at a program that uses RND. We'll write a computer program that "simulates" the tossing of a coin eight times. We'll assume that the random numbers are evenly distributed between 0 and 1. Since there are two possible results of a coin toss (HEAD or TAIL), let's decide that if $R < .5$, it represents a HEAD, and that if $R \geq .5$, it represents a TAIL (we could just as well reverse this choice).

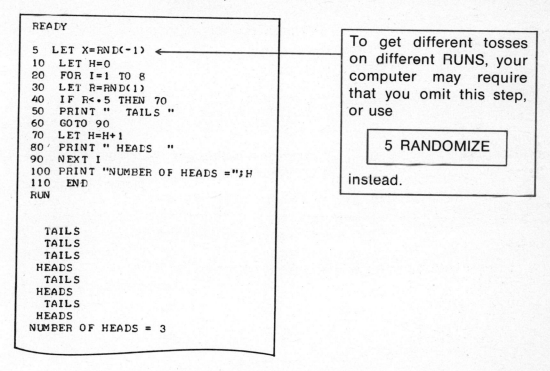

```
READY

5    LET X=RND(-1)
10   LET H=0
20   FOR I=1 TO 8
30   LET R=RND(1)
40   IF R<.5 THEN 70
50   PRINT "  TAILS "
60   GOTO 90
70   LET H=H+1
80   PRINT " HEADS  "
90   NEXT I
100  PRINT "NUMBER OF HEADS =";H
110  END
RUN


   TAILS
   TAILS
   TAILS
  HEADS
   TAILS
  HEADS
   TAILS
  HEADS
NUMBER OF HEADS = 3
```

To get different tosses on different RUNS, your computer may require that you omit this step, or use

5 RANDOMIZE

instead.

Just as if you tossed a real coin, the order of HEADS and TAILS is random. If you RUN the program several times, it is highly probable that the average number of HEADS will be approximately equal to the average number of TAILS.

Code Name: /COIN/

ON-LINE

Write a program that simulates tossing a coin 100 times. Suggestion: Put a semicolon at the end of lines 50 and 80, and add a line which prints the number of TAILS. Also experiment with changing $R < .5$ to $R <= .5$.

MAKING RND(1) MORE USEFUL

RND(1) generates decimals between 0 and 1. Frequently, though, we prefer integers between two other numbers; for instance, to simulate rolling a die, we might want to generate random integers from 1 to 6 (1, 2, 3, 4, 5, or 6).

What can we do? Well:

RND(1) gives numbers between 0 and 1 (not including 1)
6∗RND(1) gives numbers between 0 and 6 (but not including 6)
INT(6∗RND(1)) gives integers from 0 to 5.
INT(6∗RND(1)+1) gives integers from 1 to 6, which is what we wanted.

In general, INT((b+1−a)∗RND(1)+a) gives the integers from a to b inclusive. In the preceding example, a=1, b=6, and we have:

$$INT((6+1-1)*RND(1)+1)$$

MINI-EXERCISES

Write programs that each generate 10 random integers of the following kinds:

1. Integers from 5 to 20 inclusive
2. Integers from 9 to 15 inclusive
3. Integers from 1 to 3 inclusive
4. Integers from 1 to 100 inclusive
5. Integers from −50 to 50 inclusive

Code Name: /RAND/

Try the solution to Exercise (1) ON-LINE:

```
READY

5   LET X=RND(-1)     (SEE PAGE 116.)
10    FOR I=1 TO 10
20    PRINT INT(16*RND(1)+5);
30    NEXT I
40    END
RUN
```

Write a program that simulates the throwing of two dice. It should look like this:

```
RUN

FIRST DIE          SECOND DIE          TOTAL
   3                   2                 5
   2                   3                 5
   1                   3                 4
   4                   1                 5
   1                   5                 6
   4                   2                 6
   5                   2                 7
   6                   3                 9
   4                   4                 8
   2                   3                 5

END
```

Code Name: //GUESS//

Write a program that asks two players to guess which number between 1 and 100 the computer randomly picked. The program should give 10 points to the player who was closest. It might look like this:

```
RUN


PLAYER 1? 47
PLAYER 2? 78
THE COMPUTER HAD 82.
PLAYER 2 WAS CLOSEST.
SCORE:   PLAYER 1 HAS 0 POINTS; PLAYER 2 HAS 10 POINTS.

LET'S TRY AGAIN.
PLAYER 1? 31
PLAYER 2? 9
```

ON-LINE ON-LINE ON-LINE ON-LINE ON-LINE ON-LINE ON-LINE

3–7 | GOTO ... OF ... | or | ON ... GOTO ... |

Let's imagine that we are writing an American history quiz program — the computer asks multiple choice questions, the person types in the number of his choice, and then the computer not only tells him if he is right or wrong, but also why.

A sample question is:

Who was the first man to walk on the moon?
There are four choices:

1) Alan Shepard
2) John Glenn
3) Neil Armstrong
4) Buzz Aldrin

Let's call the person's answer X. He will type either a 1, 2, 3, or 4 for X.

We could then say:

```
208 IF X=1 THEN 220
209 IF X=2 THEN 230
210 IF X=3 THEN 240
211 IF X=4 THEN 250
```

These send the computer to special places in the program which tell the person why his specific answer was right or wrong.

But in BASIC, we could condense those four lines into one line:

```
210 GOTO X OF 220, 230, 240, 250
```

NOTE: On some computers, this same kind of statement is written slightly differently and is known as an ON statement — we'll explain the ON statement on page 121.

When the computer reaches line 210, it has a value of X (typed in by the person).

Line 210 says: If X=1, the computer will go to the *first* line numbered, or line 220. If X=2, the computer will go to the *second,* or 230. If X=3, it will go to the *third,* or 240. If X=4, it will go to the *fourth,* or 250.

In other words, the statement can be read like this: GOTO the Xth line number OF these __,__,__,__.

Notice that for each wrong answer, there was a separate message, explaining why it was wrong.

Now, let's finish our example, and then fill in a few more details.

Remember, the following could be part of a larger program.

```
READY

200    PRINT "WHO WAS THE FIRST MAN TO WALK ON THE MOON?"
201    PRINT "1) ALAN SHEPARD"
202    PRINT "2) JOHN GLENN"
203    PRINT "3) NEIL ARMSTRONG"
204    PRINT "4) BUZZ ALDRIN"
205    INPUT X
210    GOTO X OF 220,230,240,250
215    PRINT "PLEASE TYPE IN 1, 2, 3, OR 4."
216    GOTO 205
220    PRINT "NO, SHEPARD WAS THE FIRST AMERICAN TO GO INTO"
221    PRINT " SPACE; ARMSTRONG IS THE ANSWER."
225    GOTO 270
230    PRINT "WRONG; GLENN WAS THE FIRST AMERICAN TO ORBIT THE"
231    PRINT " EARTH; ARMSTRONG IS THE ANSWER."
235    GOTO 270
240    PRINT "RIGHT!!  ON JULY 20, 1969, ARMSTRONG BECAME THE"
241    PRINT " FIRST MAN TO WALK ON THE MOON."
245    GOTO 270
250    PRINT "NO; ALDRIN WAS THE SECOND MAN--ABOUT HALF AN HOUR"
251    PRINT " AFTER ARMSTRONG."
270    END

END
RUN


WHO WAS THE FIRST MAN TO WALK ON THE MOON?
1) ALAN SHEPARD
2) JOHN GLENN
3) NEIL ARMSTRONG
4) BUZZ ALDRIN
?3
RIGHT!!  ON JULY 20, 1969, ARMSTRONG BECAME THE
 FIRST MAN TO WALK ON THE MOON.
```

If the person types less than a 1 or more than a 4, the computer will go to line 215, which reminds the person of the rules.

In a longer program, this would be the next question.

THE ON . . . GOTO . . . STATEMENT: Many computers use the key words

ON . . . GOTO . . .   instead of   GOTO . . . OF . . . .

The ON . . . GOTO . . . statement looks like this:

210 ON X GOTO 220, 230, 240, 250

Again, if X is 1, the computer will go to the 1st line number or 220, if X is 2 to line 230, and so on.

So, the two possible forms are:

210 GOTO X OF 220, 230, 240, 250

or

210 ON X GOTO 220, 230, 240, 250

Check, perhaps by trying them on your computer, or by reading your computer manual, which form your computer uses. They do exactly the same thing.

In either case, if X is not a whole number, the value of X is truncated (the decimal part of X is chopped off). For example, IF X=3.65, a GOTO-X-OF statement will use 3 as X. If X is less than 1 OR greater than the number of lines listed, the computer will skip the GOTO-X-OF statement and continue on the *next* statement.

Finally, expressions can be used instead of X — just make sure the expression takes on the correct integer values for the number of line numbers following it. Check these examples:

20 GOTO M OF 20,30,40,50,60	20 ON M GOTO 20,30,40,50,60
80 GOTO F+Z OF 100,120,153	80 ON F+Z GOTO 100,120,153
114 GOTO P−Q OF 600,200,1800,2200	114 ON P−Q GOTO 600,200,1800,2200

These are all correct uses of GOTO...OF...or of ON... GOTO...

Code Name: /MELODY/

Use RND and GOTO K OF to write a program which generates 8 bars (measures) of melody as follows: Begin with "DO RE MI," end with "MI RE DO," and generate randomly 6 bars in between.

```
RUN

DO RE MI
RE FA MI
SOL FA MI
RE FA MI
SOL FA MI
MI SOL FA
SOL FA MI
MI RE DO
```

HINT: Try this short program to get some ideas:

```
REALY

5    LET X=RND(-1)    (SEE PAGE 116.)
10   LET K=INT(3*RND(1)+1)
20   GOTO K OF 30, 50, 70
30   PRINT "RE FA MI"
40   GOTO 10
50   PRINT "MI SOL FA"
60   GOTO 10
70   PRINT "SOL FA MI"
80   GOTO 10
90   END
RUN
```

After you have RUN the program, write the melody out in three-quarter time, using regular musical notation as shown in the diagram above.

3–3 Two-dimensional Arrays

A new mayor of Ashbank has just been elected. One of his main campaign promises was to make Ashbank a safe place in which to live.

His first directive is to the police department — cut down the number of traffic accidents. So the police commissioner's first move is an order to his computing division — get statistics on the number of accidents at each intersection.

Let's look at a map of downtown Ashbank and help ABC (The Ashbank Bureau of Computing) analyze the problem:

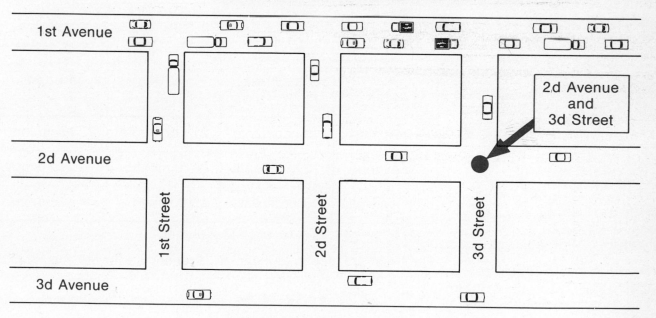

First, we'll need an easy way to refer to a particular intersection. Second, we'll have to be able to associate the number of accidents at the intersection with the name of the intersection.

We could letter the intersections with single letters, or we could use subscripted variables. Which shall it be? Well, the downtown area is rapidly expanding — so our method should make it easy to add other intersections in the future. Also, the streets already have numbers — why not use them?

With these facts in mind, we could refer to the intersections by first giving the AVENUE name, and then giving the intersecting STREET name. The intersection in our picture marked with a heavy dot is "2d AVE and 3d ST."

This suggests that it would be nice to have a second type of subscripted variable, one that has *two* subscripts. Here's what these variables look like in BASIC:

> N($2,3$) represents the number of accidents at 2d AVE and 3d ST. N($1,2$) represents the number of accidents at 1st AVE and 2d ST and so on.

Just as with single-subscript variables, the double-subscript variables store values. So if, in the past year, 23 accidents have taken place at 2d AVE and 3d ST, we can say:

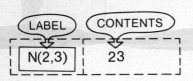

> LET N(2,3)=23

If 21 occurred at 1st AVE and 2d ST, we can say:

> LET N(1,2)=21

We can think of these storage locations as if they were arranged in a table. The *contents* are the numbers of accidents at each intersection.

Street / Avenue	1st Street	2d Street	3d Street
1st Avenue	46 accidents	21 accidents	72 accidents
2d Avenue	13 accidents	28 accidents	23 accidents
3d Avenue	16 accidents	18 accidents	34 accidents

The usual practice is to enter these numbers into the computer by rows, that is, in the order:

> 46, 21, 72, 13, 28, 23, 16, 18, 34

The best way to compare the safety of the different intersections is to find each intersection's percentage of the total accidents in Ashbank. If we found, for instance, that one intersection has 37%, and another has 21%, then it would be clear that the former for some reason is much more dangerous.

So we write the program shown on the next page.

In this example, lines 170 to 410 present four *different* quiz questions. The subroutine always does the same thing: it allows the student to input an answer, it checks the answer, and it keeps score. Notice that the correct answer is always found in the variable A.

Summary: At a GOSUB statement, the computer:
- goes to the subroutine,
- works through the subroutine until it finds a RETURN statement,
- then it branches back to the statement *right after* the GOSUB that sent it to the subroutine in the first place.

Here's a RUN of our program:

```
RUN


IN THIS PROGRAM, YOU WILL BE ASKED FOUR QUESTIONS.

AFTER EACH QUESTION, TYPE THE NUMBER OF THE ANSWER
YOU BELIEVE TO BE CORRECT.

1. ONE OF THE LONGEST CASES OF HICCOUGHING LASTED:
          1) 3 DAYS                    3) 8 WEEKS
          2) 2 WEEKS                   4) 8 YEARS
TYPE THE NUMBER OF YOUR ANSWER:?1
NO, THE ANSWER IS NUMBER 4.

2. THE LARGEST DISH EVER PREPARED WAS:
          1) FRIED ELEPHANT            3) BOILED HIPPO
          2) ROAST CAMEL               4) BAKED RHINO
TYPE THE NUMBER OF YOUR ANSWER:?1
NO, THE ANSWER IS NUMBER 2.

3. ROBERTO CLEMENTE LAST PLAYED FOR WHAT TEAM?
          1) CHICAGO                   3) ST. LOUIS
          2) PITTSBURGH                4) BOSTON
TYPE THE NUMBER OF YOUR ANSWER:?2
WOW--THAT'S RIGHT.

4. 'LOVE' IS A TERM IN WHAT SPORT?
          1) GOLF                      3) BILLIARDS
          2) SOCCER                    4) TENNIS
TYPE THE NUMBER OF YOUR ANSWER:?4
WOW--THAT'S RIGHT.

THAT'S ALL THE QUESTIONS FOR NOW.
OUT OF FOUR QUESTIONS YOU ANSWERED 2 CORRECTLY
AND 2 INCORRECTLY.
```

Code Name: /FACT QUIZ/

Write a quiz program using your own questions (and answers).

Code Name: //SUPER QUIZ//

Get 8 students to work on a longer quiz with each person contributing 3 questions. Student #1 should use line numbers in the 1000's and student #2 in the 2000's, and so on.

ON-LINE

4

Far Away Places

Twenty key words, seven commands, and four functions — that's the total count for the BASIC vocabulary studied in the first three parts of this book. Here they are:

KEY WORDS			COMMANDS	FUNCTIONS
PRINT	STOP	READ	RUN	SQR
END	FOR	DATA	LIST	INT
LET	NEXT	RESTORE	SCR	ABS
INPUT	STEP	GOTO K OF	BYE	RND
GOTO	DIM	(or ON K GOTO)	PUNCH	
IF	REM	GOSUB	TAPE	
THEN	TAB	RETURN	KEY	

As we are about to see, that's more than enough vocabulary to write programs that solve professional-level problems — to do what is called *applications* programming. Some of these applications may seem far away from the life of a student, but they will become familiar in short order.

NOTE: Since all the required features of BASIC have been explained in the first three parts of this book, we will not explain the programs in this part in complete detail. This means that it may take several days of study and ON-LINE experimentation to completely master a given programming idea. The "suggested explorations" given following the programs could take even longer. Don't be discouraged by this; that's what being a professional is all about.

A teacher and class may decide to attack the different sections of Part 4 as individualized (or team) projects. If this is the case, the list on the next page will help in selecting projects.

Here are the programs you'll find in Part 4. The sections shown here can be taken in any order; it's also OK to skip over sections in case you are in a class that's using an "individualized project" approach.

4-1 Data Analysis

/HOTEL/ and /AIRLINE/ illustrate computer reservation systems, one of the fastest growing applications of computers today.

4-2 Nonnumeric Applications

Computers can be used to manipulate words as well as numbers. The programs /SOAP/ and /MENU/ show you how.

4-3 Games and Simulations

The program /SLOT MACHINE/ makes the computer simulate a gambling device; you'll see why it's impossible to "beat the house." The program /BURIED TREASURE/ is a two-dimensional game that shows what a powerful tool coordinate geometry can be.

4-4 Business Applications

/ADD-ON INT/ and /UNPAID-BAL INT/ show you how to calculate the interest charged by credit companies and banks when they loan you money; /PAYROLL/ is a program that calculates the "take-home" pay for each employee in a company.

4-5 Batch-Mode Computing

This section is for people who use card input instead of a terminal.

4-1 Data Analysis

There are many hotels that use computers to find out if a room is available on the dates requested by a customer. Airlines use similar systems to find out if there is room on a specified flight on a specified date. There are even computer reservation systems for checking theater and sporting event ticket requests. All these systems use the same general programming idea — they compare the customer's request with data about the rooms (or seats) already reserved.

Program 1: /HOTEL RESERV/

Here are two sample RUNS of the program.

```
RUN


THE PIXIE HOTEL AUTOMATED RESERVATION SYSTEM
*********************************************

HOW MANY DAYS DO YOU WISH TO STAY?3
TYPE IN EACH DATE DESIRED AFTER EACH '?', TYPING
     MARCH 1 AS 3.01, DECEMBER 14 AS 12.14, AND SO ON.
?4.04
?4.05
?4.06

ROOM 901 IS AVAILABLE ON DATES REQUESTED.
     RATE IS $ 18 PER DAY.

ROOM 902 IS AVAILABLE ON DATES REQUESTED.
     RATE IS $ 16 PER DAY.

ROOM 905 IS AVAILABLE ON DATES REQUESTED.
     RATE IS $ 20 PER DAY.

WHICH ROOM DO YOU WISH?901
YOUR RESERVATION IS CONFIRMED.

---------------------TEAR HERE---------------------

MEMO TO RESERVATIONS: ENTER NEW DATA FOR ROOM 901.
ADD  4.04,  4.05,  4.06 TO PRESENT DATA.

---------------------TEAR HERE---------------------


RUN


THE PIXIE HOTEL AUTOMATED RESERVATION SYSTEM
*********************************************

HOW MANY DAYS DO YOU WISH TO STAY?2
TYPE IN EACH DATE DESIRED AFTER EACH '?', TYPING
     MARCH 1 AS 3.01, DECEMBER 14 AS 12.14, AND SO ON.
?4.08
?4.09

SORRY, NO ROOMS ARE AVAILABLE FOR ALL DAYS REQUESTED.

---------------------TEAR HERE---------------------
```

The data on hotel rooms are given in DATA statements that use the following code, or *structure*:

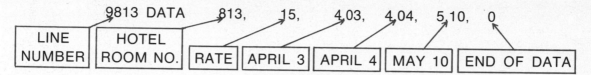

| LINE NUMBER | HOTEL ROOM NO. | RATE | APRIL 3 | APRIL 4 | MAY 10 | END OF DATA |

9813 DATA   813,   15,   4.03,   4.04,   5.10,   0

This statement says that Room 813 rents for $15 per day, and that it is *already reserved* for April 3, April 4, and May 10. The zero at the end is a "flag" to the computer that lets it know there is no more information on file for Room 813.

A LISTing of the program is given below.

```
10    PRINT "THE PIXIE HOTEL AUTOMATED RESERVATION SYSTEM"
20    PRINT "**********************************************"
30    PRINT
40    PRINT "HOW MANY DAYS DO YOU WISH TO STAY";
50    INPUT N
60    PRINT "TYPE IN EACH DATE DESIRED AFTER EACH '?', TYPING"
70    PRINT "      MARCH 1 AS 3.01, DECEMBER 14 AS 12.14, AND SO ON."
80    FOR I=1 TO N
90    INPUT D[I]
100   NEXT I
110   LET J=0
120   READ R
130   IF R<0 THEN 280
140   READ P
150   READ D1
160   IF D1 <> 0 THEN 210
170   LET J=J+1
180   LET R[J]=R
190   LET P[J]=P
200   GO TO 120
210   FOR I=1 TO N
220   IF D1=D[I] THEN 250
230   NEXT I
240   GO TO 150
250   READ D1
260   IF D1=0 THEN 120
270   GO TO 250
280   IF J <> 0 THEN 320
290   PRINT
300   PRINT "SORRY, NO ROOMS ARE AVAILABLE FOR ALL DAYS REQUESTED."
310   GO TO 500
320   PRINT
330   FOR I=1 TO J
340   PRINT "ROOM";R[I];" IS AVAILABLE ON DATES REQUESTED."
350   PRINT "     RATE IS $";P[I];" PER DAY."
360   PRINT
370   NEXT I
380   PRINT "WHICH ROOM DO YOU WISH";
390   INPUT R
400   PRINT "YOUR RESERVATION IS CONFIRMED."
410   PRINT
420   PRINT "-------------------TEAR HERE--------------------"
430   PRINT
440   PRINT "MEMO TO RESERVATIONS: ENTER NEW DATA FOR ROOM";R"."
450   PRINT "ADD ";
460   FOR I=1 TO N-1
470   PRINT D[I];", ";
480   NEXT I
490   PRINT D[N];" TO PRESENT DATA."
500   PRINT
510   PRINT "-------------------TEAR HERE--------------------"
520   FOR I=1 TO 8
530   PRINT
540   NEXT I
550   STOP
```

> This must be done by typing in new DATA statements. On computers that have file commands, the program can be written so that the computer makes its own changes in DATA.

```
560    DATA 901,18,4.08,4.1,0
570    DATA 902,16,4.03,4.08,4.09,0
580    DATA 903,17,3.01,3.02,4.04,4.05,4.08,0
590    DATA 904,14,4.03,4.04,4.09,4.1,0
600    DATA 905,20,4.08,0
610    DATA -1
620    END
```

SPECIAL INFORMATION FOR SOME COMPUTERS

NOTE: We used the code 4.03 for April 3 since all versions of BASIC allow DATA statements that use numbers. However, it may be that your computer also allows "strings" (check the index in your computer reference manual). If so, you can also store alphabetic information. Even better, if your computer allows file commands, you can use these instead of DATA statements. You'll have to read about using file commands by yourself, since they differ with every computer.

Program 2: /AIR RESERV/

This reservation program uses a slightly different method for storing and checking data. Take-A-Chance-International Airlines (TACI-Air) keeps the information on how many seats are available on each of their two daily flights in the double-subscript variables $A(I,J)$ (for flight 1) and $B(I,J)$ (for flight 2). The subscript I represents the month, and J the day of the month. Thus,

$$LET\ B(11,8)=3$$

would be a way of storing in the computer the information that there are 3 seats available on flight 2 on November 8.

TACI-Air keeps current records for two months. The following program is for January and February. The program assumes that 3 passenger seats are available on each plane at the start. Exceptions to this rule are then handled with READ-DATA statements.

Here's a sample RUN:

```
RUN


TACI-AIR RESERVATION SYSTEM
***************************

ENTER MONTH, DAY, FLIGHT NO., NO. OF SEATS DESIRED?1,18,2,2

  2 SEAT(S) CONFIRMED ON FLIGHT NO. 2 ON 1/ 18
DO YOU WISH TO TRY ANOTHER RESERVATION (TYPE 1 FOR YES,
     0 FOR NO)?1

ENTER MONTH, DAY, FLIGHT NO., NO. OF SEATS DESIRED?1,5,2,1
```

130

```
SORRY--NOT ENOUGH SEATS AVAILABLE ON THAT FLIGHT.
DO YOU WISH TO TRY ANOTHER RESERVATION (TYPE 1 FOR YES,
    0 FOR NO)?1

ENTER MONTH, DAY, FLIGHT NO., NO. OF SEATS DESIRED?1,5,1,1

 1 SEAT(S) CONFIRMED ON FLIGHT NO. 1 ON 1/ 5
DO YOU WISH TO TRY ANOTHER RESERVATION (TYPE 1 FOR YES,
    0 FOR NO)?0

------------------------------------------------------
MESSAGE TO RESERVATIONS AGENT:  ENTER NEW DATA
STATEMENT(S) BEFORE RUNNING THIS PRGRAM AGAIN.
```

Here's a LISTing of the program /AIR RESERV/.

```
10   DIM A[13,31],B[13,31]
20   FOR I=1 TO 2
30   FOR J=1 TO 31
40   LET A[I,J]=3
50   LET B[I,J]=3
60   NEXT J
70   NEXT I
80   LET A[2,29]=A[2,30]=A[2,31]=0
90   LET B[2,29]=B[2,30]=B[2,31]=0
100   READ I,J
110   IF I=13 THEN 140
120   READ A[I,J],B[I,J]
130   GOTO 100
140   PRINT "TACI-AIR RESERVATION SYSTEM"
150   PRINT "**************************"
160   PRINT
170   PRINT "ENTER MONTH, DAY, FLIGHT NO., NO. OF SEATS DESIRED";
180   INPUT M,D,F,N
190   PRINT
200   GOTO F OF 210,250
210   IF A[M,D]<N THEN 290
220   PRINT N;" SEAT(S) CONFIRMED ON FLIGHT NO.";F;" ON";M;"/";D
230   LET A[M,D]=A[M,D]-N
240   GOTO 300
250   IF B[M,D]<N THEN 290
260   PRINT N;" SEAT(S) CONFIRMED ON FLIGHT NO.";F;" ON";M;"/";D
270   LET B[M,D]=B[M,D]-N
280   GOTO 300
290   PRINT "SORRY--NOT ENOUGH SEATS AVAILABLE ON THAT FLIGHT."
300   PRINT "DO YOU WISH TO TRY ANOTHER RESERVATION (TYPE 1 FOR YES,"
310   PRINT "     0 FOR NO)";
320   INPUT A
330   IF A=1 THEN 160
340   PRINT
350   PRINT "------------------------------------------------------"
360   PRINT "MESSAGE TO RESERVATIONS AGENT:  ENTER NEW DATA"
370   PRINT "STATEMENT(S) BEFORE RUNNING THIS PROGRAM AGAIN."
380   DATA 1,2,2,2,1,3,2,1,1,4,1,1,1,5,1,0,13,13
390   END
```

These steps remove the extra days from February (not a leap year).

The first "13" stops the READ of line 100. The last "13" is needed to prevent an OUT OF DATA message.

Lines 20 to 70 put a "3" in each of the variables A(I,J) and B(I,J). This is the number of seats normally available on one of TACI's flights. Changes in this number are taken care of by the READ and DATA statements (100, 120, and 380). For example,

380 DATA 1,2,2,2

means that on January 2, flights A and B have only *two* seats left.

Suggested Explorations:

1. Add statements to /AIR RESERV/ which automatically tell the reservation agent what new DATA should be added to statement 380 before running the program again.

2. Inventory Control: Harry Hardsell is a salesman for the Ace Hardware Company. He is in Chicago and has a customer who wishes to order 7842 left-handed, brass-plated bolts, stock number 809, and 87 model-302 red buckets. Harry mutters to himself, "Oh, if only I could dial a computer at company headquarters in Oshkosh, and using my portable terminal, RUN a program that would tell me how many of each of these items are in stock for immediate delivery, the price of each, and the total bill less 5% cash discount." Can you write a program for Harry that does these things for any one of ten different products?

4-2 Nonnumeric Applications

We tend to think of computers as calculating machines which work only with numbers. This is not completely true. Computers can also do things with words and letters. We'll show two interesting examples of this that work on even the simplest minicomputers.

Program 3: /SOAP/

Have you ever wondered how names for cereals, detergents, and such are chosen? We'll probably never know, but let's see what a computer might do.

Study the print-out at the top of the next page.

```
RUN

PROGRAM TO GENERATE NAMES BEGINNING WITH 'GL'

GLAS          GLAP          GLAT          GLAR          GLAB

GLES          GLEP          GLET          GLER          GLEB

GLIS          GLIP          GLIT          GLIR          GLIB

GLOS          GLOP          GLOT          GLOR          GLOB

GLUS          GLUP          GLUT          GLUR          GLUB
```

The trick to /SOAP/ is to use nested FOR loops. Our program always starts the name of the soap with GL. It uses the FOR loop starting in line 120 to choose a vowel. It uses the FOR loop in line 130 to add each of the consonants S, P, T, R, and B. Then it goes back and tries a second vowel, and so on. Here is a LISTing:

```
100    PRINT "PROGRAM TO GENERATE NAMES BEGINNING WITH 'GL'"
110    PRINT
120    FOR I=1 TO 5
130    FOR J=1 TO 5
140    PRINT "GL";
150    GOTO I OF 160,180,200,220,240
160    PRINT "A";
170    GOTO 250
180    PRINT "E";
190    GOTO 250
200    PRINT "I";
210    GOTO 250
220    PRINT "O";
230    GOTO 250
240    PRINT "U";
250    GOTO J OF 260,280,300,320,340
260    PRINT "S",
270    GOTO 350
280    PRINT "P",
290    GOTO 350
300    PRINT "T",
310    GOTO 350
320    PRINT "R",
330    GOTO 350
340    PRINT "B",
350    NEXT J
360    NEXT I
370    END
```

Program 4: /MENU/

Let's suppose that you have just become vice-president in charge of promotion for Gus's Restaurant. You decide to introduce a novelty — a terminal at every table where a customer can custom-order his meal. An example of what might happen is shown on the next page.

```
RUN

+++ THE AUTOMATED RESTAURANT +++

THIS IS GUS'S ROBOT READY TO HELP YOU SELECT YOUR MEAL.

TYPE THE NUMBER OF YOUR SELECTION AFTER EACH '?'.

1=TOMATO JUICE(.15),2=GRAPEFRUIT(.30),3=CLAM CHOWDER(.40)?2
1=HAMBURGER(.60),2=CHEESEBURGER(.70),3=HOT DOG(.50)?3
1=MUSTARD(.00),2=CATSUP(.00),3=NOTHING?1
1=APPLE PIE(.30),2=ICE CREAM(.20),3=CHOCOLATE CAKE(.25)?3
1=COFFEE(.15),2=SOFT DRINK(.15),3=MILK(.15)?1


ORDER TO COOK:  A 2,  E 3,  C 1,  D 3,  B 1


****** ANNOUNCING ---
    YOUR CUSTOM-TAILORED DINNER

STARTING WITH
**++ SWEET PINK-CENTERED GRAPEFRUIT

AND FEATURING
++** A SUCCULENT HOT DOG SMOTHERED WITH MUSTARD

AND FOR DESSERT
**RICH MOIST CHOCOLATE CAKE

DOWNED WITH
*FRESH-BREWED COFFEE


OH, YES, YOUR BILL IS $ 1.2.
YOUR SUGGESTED TIP IS $ .18.

VERY NICE SERVING YOU. COME AGAIN.
```

Here is a LISTing of /MENU/.

```
10    PRINT "+++ THE AUTOMATED RESTAURANT +++"
20    PRINT
30    PRINT "THIS IS GUS'S ROBOT READY TO HELP YOU SELECT YOUR MEAL."
40    PRINT
50    PRINT "TYPE THE NUMBER OF YOUR SELECTION AFTER EACH '?'."
60    PRINT
70    PRINT "1=TOMATO JUICE(.15),2=GRAPEFRUIT(.30),3=CLAM CHOWDER(.40)";
80    INPUT A
90    PRINT "1=HAMBURGER(.60),2=CHEESEBURGER(.70),3=HOT DOG(.50)";
100   INPUT E
110   PRINT "1=MUSTARD(.00),2=CATSUP(.00),3=NOTHING";
120   INPUT C
130   PRINT "1=APPLE PIE(.30),2=ICE CREAM(.20),3=CHOCOLATE CAKE(.25)";
140   INPUT D
150   PRINT "1=COFFEE(.15),2=SOFT DRINK(.15),3=MILK(.15)";
160   INPUT B
170   PRINT
180   PRINT
190   PRINT "ORDER TO COOK:  A";A;",  E";E;",  C";C;",  D";D;",  B";B
200   PRINT
210   PRINT
220   LET P=0
230   PRINT "****** ANNOUNCING ---"
240   PRINT "   YOUR CUSTOM-TAILORED DINNER"
250   PRINT
```

```
260    PRINT "STARTING WITH"
270    GOTO A OF 280,310,340
280    PRINT "**++ TANTALIZING TOMATO JUICE"
290    LET P=P+.15
300    GOTO 360
310    PRINT "**++ SWEET PINK-CENTERED GRAPEFRUIT"
320    LET P=P+.3
330    GOTO 360
340    PRINT "**++ DELICIOUS CLAM CHOWDER"
350    LET P=P+.4
360    PRINT
370    PRINT "AND FEATURING"
380    GOTO E OF 390,420,450
390    PRINT "+++* A SIZZLING HAMBURGER";
400    LET P=P+.6
410    GOTO 470
420    PRINT "+++* A SIZZLING CHEESEBURGER";
430    LET P=P+.7
440    GOTO 470
450    PRINT "+++* A SUCCULENT HOT DOG";
460    LET P=P+.5
470    GOTO C OF 480,500,520
480    PRINT " SMOTHERED WITH MUSTARD"
490    GOTO 530
500    PRINT " SMOTHERED WITH CATSUP"
510    GOTO 530
520    PRINT
530    PRINT
540    PRINT "AND FOR DESSERT"
550    GOTO D OF 560,590,620
560    PRINT "**MOTHER'S APPLE PIE"
570    LET P=P+.3
580    GOTO 640
590    PRINT "**CREAMY ICE CREAM"
600    LET P=P+.2
610    GOTO 640
620    PRINT "**RICH MOIST CHOCOLATE CAKE"
630    LET P=P+.25
640    PRINT
650    PRINT "DOWNED WITH"
660    GOTO B OF 670,700,730
670    PRINT "*FRESH-BREWED COFFEE"
680    LET P=P+.15
690    GOTO 750
700    PRINT "*REFRESHING SOFT DRINK"
710    LET P=P+.15
720    GOTO 750
730    PRINT "*WHOLESOME VITAMIN-ENRICHED MILK"
740    LET P=P+.15
750    PRINT
760    PRINT
770    PRINT "OH, YES, YOUR BILL IS $";P;"."
780    LET P1=INT((P*.15+.005)*100)/100
790    PRINT "YOUR SUGGESTED TIP IS $";P1;"."
800    PRINT
810    PRINT "VERY NICE SERVING YOU. COME AGAIN."
820    END
```

Suggested Explorations:

1. Write a program that will generate names for musical groups. For example, you might generate names by combining adjectives, colors, and animals (producing such names as HAPPY PURPLE CHICKEN, OUTRAGEOUS ORANGE OSTRICH).

2. Write a program that produces sentences of the form
   THE (noun) (verb) (adverb).

4-3 Games and Simulations

Although many people think of games as being used only for recreation, computer games can also serve serious purposes. For example, computer scientists have programmed games like chess in order to study the question of "machine intelligence." Simulations (programs that imitate something) are often combined with games to help study complex ideas.

Program 5: /SLOT MACHINE/

This program simulates (acts like) a machine that has 3 "windows." A picture of an orange, a lemon, or a cherry appears in each window each time you put in money (50 cents in our machine) and pull the imaginary handle. If all three pictures are the same, you win $3.00. If not, you lose your 50 cents.

One way of figuring your odds for winning is to draw a diagram like that shown at the left below. The winning combinations are marked with the symbol ★. You can see that although there are 27 possible combinations, only 3 of these are "winners."

Here are all the 27 possible paths;† the "winning" combinations are ringed.

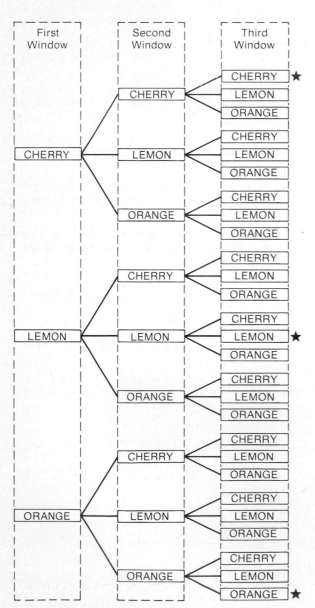

(CCC)	CCL	CCO
CLC	CLL	CLO
COC	COL	COO
LCC	LCL	LCO
LLC	(LLL)	LLO
LOC	LOL	LOO
OCC	OCL	OCO
OLC	OLL	OLO
OOC	OOL	(OOO)

A mathematician would say that your probability of winning on this machine is:

$$P = \frac{\text{No. of winning combinations}}{\text{No. of possible combinations}} = \frac{3}{27} = \frac{1}{9}$$

In other words, if you played 90 times, you would win about $\frac{1}{9}$ of the time, or 10 times.

Playing 90 times would cost you $45.
Winning 10 times would give you $30.

So you can see that on the average the owner of the machine would make $15 on every 90 plays. In other words, in the long run, on this machine you lose, he wins. A sample RUN of this program is given on the next page.

† Challenge: Write a program that will print out this list.

```
RUN

THIS IS A $.50 SLOT MACHINE.
PAYOFF IS $3 FOR 3 CHERRIES, 3 LEMONS, OR 3 ORANGES.
ALL OTHER COMBINATIONS LOSE.
HOW MANY 50-CENT PIECES DO YOU WANT TO USE IN PLAY?6
YOU START WITH $ 3
DO YOU WISH TO PLAY (TYPE 1 FOR YES, 0 FOR NO)?1
$$$ORANGE$$$$###LEMON######LEMON###   TOO BAD--YOU LOST $.50.

YOU NOW HAVE $ 2.5
DO YOU WISH TO PLAY (TYPE 1 FOR YES, 0 FOR NO)?1
$$$ORANGE$$$$$$ORANGE$$$***CHERRY***   TOO BAD--YOU LOST $.50.

YOU NOW HAVE $ 2
DO YOU WISH TO PLAY (TYPE 1 FOR YES, 0 FOR NO)?1
###LEMON######LEMON######LEMON###   GREAT--YOU WON $3.

YOU NOW HAVE $ 5
DO YOU WISH TO PLAY (TYPE 1 FOR YES, 0 FOR NO)?1
$$$ORANGE$$$###LEMON######LEMON###   TOO BAD--YOU LOST $.50.

YOU NOW HAVE $ 4.5
DO YOU WISH TO PLAY (TYPE 1 FOR YES, 0 FOR NO)?1
###LEMON###$$$ORANGE$$$$$$ORANGE$$$   TOO BAD--YOU LOST $.50.

YOU NOW HAVE $ 4
DO YOU WISH TO PLAY (TYPE 1 FOR YES, 0 FOR NO)?1
***CHERRY***$$$ORANGE$$$$$$ORANGE$$$   TOO BAD--YOU LOST $.50.

YOU NOW HAVE $ 3.5
DO YOU WISH TO PLAY (TYPE 1 FOR YES, 0 FOR NO)?1
***CHERRY***$$$ORANGE$$$$$$ORANGE$$$   TOO BAD--YOU LOST $.50.

YOU NOW HAVE $ 3
DO YOU WISH TO PLAY (TYPE 1 FOR YES, 0 FOR NO)?1
###LEMON###***CHERRY***$$$ORANGE$$$   TOO BAD--YOU LOST $.50.

YOU NOW HAVE $ 2.5
DO YOU WISH TO PLAY (TYPE 1 FOR YES, 0 FOR NO)?1
###LEMON###$$$ORANGE$$$###LEMON###   TOO BAD--YOU LOST $.50.

YOU NOW HAVE $ 2
DO YOU WISH TO PLAY (TYPE 1 FOR YES, 0 FOR NO)?1
###LEMON###***CHERRY***$$$ORANGE$$$   TOO BAD--YOU LOST $.50.

YOU NOW HAVE $ 1.5
DO YOU WISH TO PLAY (TYPE 1 FOR YES, 0 FOR NO)?1
###LEMON###$$$ORANGE$$$###LEMON###   TOO BAD--YOU LOST $.50.

YOU NOW HAVE $ 1
DO YOU WISH TO PLAY (TYPE 1 FOR YES, 0 FOR NO)?1
$$$ORANGE$$$###LEMON###***CHERRY***   TOO BAD--YOU LOST $.50.

YOU NOW HAVE $ .5
DO YOU WISH TO PLAY (TYPE 1 FOR YES, 0 FOR NO)?1
###LEMON###***CHERRY***$$$ORANGE$$$   TOO BAD--YOU LOST $.50.

YOU HAVE LOST ALL YOUR MONEY.
SORRY ABOUT THAT
```

To simulate selecting one of the three "pictures," we use the BASIC statement (see page 138):

160 LET N=INT(3*RND(I))+1

This gives us a 1, a 2, or a 3 for N. Then by using

170 GOTO N OF 180, 210, 240
(or 170 ON N GOTO 180, 210, 240 on some computers)

our program branches to a line that prints one of the words "CHERRY," "LEMON," or "ORANGE."

Here's a LISTing of the program for you to study.

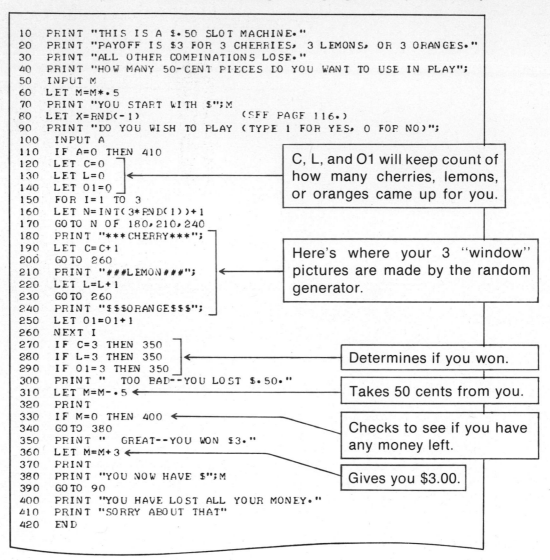

```
10   PRINT "THIS IS A $.50 SLOT MACHINE."
20   PRINT "PAYOFF IS $3 FOR 3 CHERRIES, 3 LEMONS, OR 3 ORANGES."
30   PRINT "ALL OTHER COMBINATIONS LOSE."
40   PRINT "HOW MANY 50-CENT PIECES DO YOU WANT TO USE IN PLAY";
50   INPUT M
60   LET M=M*.5
70   PRINT "YOU START WITH $";M
80   LET X=RND(-1)                    (SEE PAGE 116.)
90   PRINT "DO YOU WISH TO PLAY (TYPE 1 FOR YES, 0 FOR NO)";
100  INPUT A
110  IF A=0 THEN 410
120  LET C=0
130  LET L=0
140  LET O1=0
150  FOR I=1 TO 3
160  LET N=INT(3*RND(1))+1
170  GOTO N OF 180,210,240
180  PRINT "***CHERRY***";
190  LET C=C+1
200  GOTO 260
210  PRINT "###LEMON###";
220  LET L=L+1
230  GOTO 260
240  PRINT "$$$ORANGE$$$";
250  LET O1=O1+1
260  NEXT I
270  IF C=3 THEN 350
280  IF L=3 THEN 350
290  IF O1=3 THEN 350
300  PRINT "   TOO BAD--YOU LOST $.50."
310  LET M=M-.5
320  PRINT
330  IF M=0 THEN 400
340  GOTO 380
350  PRINT "   GREAT--YOU WON $3."
360  LET M=M+3
370  PRINT
380  PRINT "YOU NOW HAVE $";M
390  GOTO 90
400  PRINT "YOU HAVE LOST ALL YOUR MONEY."
410  PRINT "SORRY ABOUT THAT"
420  END
```

C, L, and O1 will keep count of how many cherries, lemons, or oranges came up for you.

Here's where your 3 "window" pictures are made by the random generator.

Determines if you won.

Takes 50 cents from you.

Checks to see if you have any money left.

Gives you $3.00.

Program 6: /BURIED TREASURE/

To play this game you need a 10 by 10 grid like the one shown at the top of the next page. The computer will randomly select a rectangular block of 4 adjacent squares (horizontally or vertically) to represent a "buried treasure." You are to try to locate it by "digging holes." The remaining instructions are given in the program. A sample RUN is given on the next page.

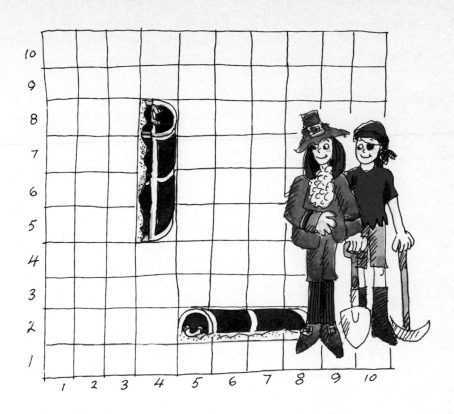

```
RUN


YOU WILL NEED A 10 BY 10 GRID TO REFER TO IN PLAYING THIS GAME.
THE COMPUTER HAS BURIED A 'TREASURE' IN A FOUR-SQUARE
 RECTANGULAR REGION WITHIN THE GRID.  YOU CAN DIG 10
  TEST HOLES IN AN AFTERNOON.  YOU REPRESENT THE LOCA-
  TION OF EACH HOLE BY TYPING AN X-COORDINATE, A COMMA,
  AND A Y-COORDINATE.


WHERE DO YOU WANT YOUR FIRST HOLE?1,1
NOTHING THERE--NO. OF TRIES LEFT:   9

NEXT HOLE?2,2
NOTHING THERE--NO. OF TRIES LEFT:   8

NEXT HOLE?3,3
NOTHING THERE--NO. OF TRIES LEFT:   7

NEXT HOLE?4,4
NOTHING THERE--NO. OF TRIES LEFT:   6

NEXT HOLE?5,5
NOTHING THERE--NO. OF TRIES LEFT:   5

NEXT HOLE?6,6
NOTHING THERE--NO. OF TRIES LEFT:   4

NEXT HOLE?7,7
EUREKA--YOU FOUND IT!
```

A LISTing of this program is given on the next page.

Here's a LISTing of this program for you to study.

```
10    PRINT "YOU WILL NEED A 10 BY 10 GRID TO REFER TO IN PLAYING";
20    PRINT " THIS GAME."
30    PRINT "THE COMPUTER HAS BURIED A 'TREASURE' IN A FOUR-SQUARE"
40    PRINT " RECTANGULAR REGION WITHIN THE GRID.  YOU CAN DIG 10"
50    PRINT " TEST HOLES IN AN AFTERNOON.  YOU REPRESENT THE LOCA-"
60    PRINT " TION OF EACH HOLE BY TYPING AN X-COORDINATE, A COMMA,"
70    PRINT " AND A Y-COORDINATE."
80    PRINT
90    LET X=RND(-1)
100   LET Z=INT(2*RND(1)+1)
110   GOTO Z OF 120,190
120   LET X[1]=INT(7*RND(1)+1)
130   LET Y[1]=INT(10*RND(1)+1)
140   FOR I=2 TO 4
150   LET X[I]=X[I-1]+1
160   LET Y[I]=Y[I-1]
170   NEXT I
180   GOTO 250
190   LET X[1]=INT(10*RND(1)+1)
200   LET Y[1]=INT(7*RND(1)+1)
210   FOR I=2 TO 4
220   LET X[I]=X[I-1]
230   LET Y[I]=Y[I-1]+1
240   NEXT I
250   LET S=10
260   PRINT
270   PRINT "WHERE DO YOU WANT YOUR FIRST HOLE";
280   INPUT X,Y
290   FOR I=1 TO 4
300   IF X <> X[I] THEN 320
310   IF Y=Y[I] THEN 470
320   NEXT I
330   PRINT "NOTHING THERE--";
340   LET S=S-1
350   IF S=0 THEN 400
360   PRINT "NO. OF TRIES LEFT: ";S
370   PRINT
380   PRINT "NEXT HOLE";
390   GOTO 280
400   PRINT "TIME TO GO HOME"
410   PRINT "THE TREASURE WAS LOCATED AT ";
420   FOR I=1 TO 3
430   PRINT "(";X[I];",";Y[I];"), ";
440   NEXT I
450   PRINT " AND (";X[4];",";Y[4];")."
460   STOP
470   PRINT "EUREKA--YOU FOUND IT!"
480   END
```

NOTE: Our coordinates for this problem differ from the usual Cartesian coordinates, which name *points*. Our coordinates identify squares.

Challenge: If you increase the number of tries to 16, can you devise a strategy that will always win?

Suggested Explorations:

1. Write a program that plays another game. If you need ideas, see if your library has a copy of *Game Playing with Computers* by Donald D. Spencer (Spartan, 1968).

2. Modify /BURIED TREASURE/ so that when you have missed, the computer tells you whether your X- and Y-coordinates were too large or too small. What is the minimum number of tries you now need to insure winning?

4–4 Business Applications

More and more business operations are being handled with the aid of computers. In this section we'll look at some applications that involve the financial side of business.

Let's suppose that you want to start your own business. To get started, you'll have to borrow money. The "rent" that you'll have to pay on your loan is called *interest*. Interest is calculated by multiplying the amount borrowed, by the interest *rate* per year, and then multiplying this answer by the number of years you wish to borrow the money. (Interest rates are usually given as a percent per year.)

EXAMPLE: Suppose that you borrow $1,000 at 8% per year for two years. How much "rent" (interest) must be paid?

$$1000 \quad * \quad .08 \quad * \quad 2 \quad = \quad 80*2=\$160$$

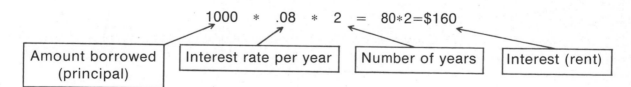

| Amount borrowed (principal) | Interest rate per year | Number of years | Interest (rent) |

Of course, in addition to paying the $160 interest, you'll also have to pay back the $1,000! Now comes the catch — you'll be expected to pay this back in monthly installments, starting right away (not 2 years from now).

Question: Even though I start paying back the money I borrowed right away, do I have to pay interest on the *full* amount? The answer is usually *yes*. Let's see how this works.

"Add-on" interest is charged by most finance companies. This means that the interest is added to the principal right away, and that you then pay back this *total* amount in monthly installments. Here's a program that calculates the monthly installments for a loan of $18,000, paid back over 5 years (60 months) at the rate of 6.5% per year "add-on" interest.

```
RUN


INSTALLMENT PAYMENTS WITH ADD-ON INTEREST

AMOUNT BORROWED (PRINCIPAL) =?18000
ANNUAL INTEREST RATE (DECIMAL) =?.065
NUMBER OF MONTHS TO REPAY THE LOAN =?60

YOU PAY $ 397.5 EACH MONTH FOR THE NEXT 60 MONTHS.
INTEREST YOU ARE PAYING EACH MONTH IS $ 97.5

AT THE END OF 5 YEARS:

PRINCIPAL REPAID     TOTAL INTEREST        SUM OF THE PAYMENTS
  18000                  5850                  23850
```

The total interest is computed by using this formula:

Total interest=(Principal)(Interest rate)(No. of years)

The monthly installment is found as follows:

$$\text{Monthly installment}=\frac{\text{Principal}+\text{Total interest}}{\text{No. of months}}$$

You will find these formulas in lines 100 and 110 of the following program:

```
10    PRINT "INSTALLMENT PAYMENTS WITH ADD-ON INTEREST"
20    PRINT
30    PRINT "AMOUNT BORROWED (PRINCIPAL) =";
40    INPUT P
50    PRINT "ANNUAL INTEREST RATE (DECIMAL) =";
60    INPUT I
70    PRINT "NUMBER OF MONTHS TO REPAY THE LOAN =";
80    INPUT M
90    PRINT
100   LET T=P*I*(M/12)
110   LET M1=(P+T)/M
120   LET I1=T/M
130   PRINT "YOU PAY $";M1;" EACH MONTH FOR THE NEXT";M;" MONTHS."
140   PRINT "INTEREST YOU ARE PAYING EACH MONTH IS $";I1
150   PRINT
160   PRINT "AT THE END OF";M/12;" YEARS:"
170   PRINT
180   PRINT "PRINCIPAL REPAID"; TAB(20); "TOTAL INTEREST";
190   PRINT TAB(40);"SUM OF THE PAYMENTS"
200   PRINT P; TAB(20); T; TAB(40);M*M1
210   END
```

Notice that in /ADD-ON/ the borrower paid five years' interest on the *full* amount borrowed, even though he began paying part of it back each month.

On large loans to well-established companies, banks sometimes compute the interest on only the *unpaid balance* (amount still owed). This is a more complicated calculation, and the computer can be a real help.

Program 8: /UNPAID-BAL INT/

Let's now look at the RUN of a program that calculates the monthly payments on an $18,000 five-year loan at 6.5% interest computed on the *unpaid balance* for each month. Our program has the extra feature of showing how to split the payments (shares) among several "partners" (3 in our example).

```
RUN


INSTALLMENT PAYMENTS WITH INTEREST ON UNPAID BALANCE

AMOUNT BORROWED (PRINCIPAL) =?18000
ANNUAL INTEREST RATE (DECIMAL) =?.065
NUMBER OF MONTHS TO REPAY THE LOAN =?60
NUMBER OF PARTNERS WHO BORROWED THE MONEY =?3
```

MONTH	PRINCIPAL OWED	INTEREST	MONTHLY PAYMENT	SHARE
1	18000	97.5	397.5	132.5
2	17700	95.88	395.88	131.96
3	17400	94.25	394.25	131.417
4	17100	92.63	392.63	130.877
5	16800	91	391	130.333
6	16500	89.38	389.38	129.793
7	16200	87.75	387.75	129.25
8	15900	86.13	386.13	128.71
9	15600	84.5	384.5	128.167
10	15300	82.88	382.88	127.627
11	15000	81.25	381.25	127.083
12	14700	79.63	379.63	126.543
13	14400	78	378	126
14	14100	76.38	376.38	125.46
15	13800	74.75	374.75	124.917
45	4800	26	326	108.667
46	4500	24.38	324.38	108.127
47	4200	22.75	322.75	107.583
48	3900	21.13	321.13	107.043
49	3600	19.5	319.5	106.5
50	3300	17.88	317.88	105.96
51	3000	16.25	316.25	105.417
52	2700	14.63	314.63	104.877
53	2400	13	313	104.333
54	2100	11.38	311.38	103.793
55	1800	9.75	309.75	103.25
56	1500	8.12	308.12	102.707
57	1200	6.5	306.5	102.167
58	900	4.88	304.88	101.627
59	600	3.25	303.25	101.083
60	300	1.63	301.63	100.543
TOTALS PAID		2973.86	20973.9	6991.29

You'll notice that when interest is calculated on the unpaid balance, the total interest on $18,000 over five years is $2,973.86. But (see page 142) it is $5,850 for add-on interest over five years, even though both calculations used the same rate per year (6.5%). The total add-on interest is approximately *twice* as much as the total interest paid on the unpaid balance!

143

Here is a listing of the program /UNPAID-BAL INT/:

```
10   LET T1=0
20   LET T2=0
30   LET T3=0
40   PRINT "INSTALLMENT PAYMENTS WITH INTEREST ON UNPAID BALANCE"
50   PRINT
60   PRINT "AMOUNT BORROWED (PRINCIPAL) =";
70   INPUT P
80   PRINT "ANNUAL INTEREST RATE (DECIMAL) =";
90   INPUT I
100  PRINT "NUMBER OF MONTHS TO REPAY THE LOAN =";
110  INPUT M
120  PRINT "NUMBER OF PARTNERS WHO BORROWED THE MONEY =";
130  INPUT N
140  PRINT
150  LET P1=INT((P/M+.005)*100)/100
160  PRINT "MONTH"; TAB(10); "PRINCIPAL OWED"; TAB(26); "INTEREST";
170  PRINT TAB(40); "MONTHLY PAYMENT"; TAB(60); "SHARE"
180  FOR J=1 TO M
190  LET I1=INT((1/12*(I*P)+.005)*100)/100
200  LET P2=P1+I1
210  LET T1=T1+I1
220  LET T2=T2+P2
230  LET Z=P2/N
240  LET T3=T3+Z
250  PRINT J; TAB(10); P; TAB(26); I1; TAB(40); P2; TAB(60); Z
260  LET P=P-P1
270  NEXT J
280  PRINT
290  PRINT "TOTALS PAID"; TAB(26); T1; TAB(40); T2; TAB(60); T
300  END
```

The calculation part of this program is done over and over (60 times) in the FOR loop of lines 180 to 270. The important line to notice is:

260 LET P=P−P1

This statement *reduces* the principal by the amount paid. This means that the interest calculation in line 190 gets smaller and smaller for each month.

> SPECIAL TRICK: The +.005 used in lines 280 and 300 causes the money to be "rounded off" to the nearest penny.
>
> EXAMPLE: 8/3=2.66667   INT((8/3+.005)*100)/100=2.67

Program 9: /PAYROLL/

Figuring out the paycheck for each employee in a big company is a lot of work, and computers are used extensively for this job. The computer also calculates tax deductions and other amounts to be subtracted from the "gross" pay of an employee. The amount left is called "net" or "take-home" pay.

Our payroll program will have to make some assumptions:

1. Employees receive their normal "hourly rate" for the first 40 hours each week. After that their rate is multiplied by 1.5 (time and a half).

2. Tax deductions are made on the following approximate basis:

GROSS WEEKLY PAY $50 OR LESS: NO TAX
GROSS WEEKLY PAY $51 TO $75:   5% TAX WITHHELD
GROSS WEEKLY PAY $76 TO $100:   10% TAX WITHHELD
GROSS WEEKLY PAY $101 TO $150:   15% TAX WITHHELD
GROSS WEEKLY PAY OVER $150:   20% TAX WITHHELD

3. Each employee is allowed to specify an amount to be taken out of his paycheck and deposited in a savings plan.

Here's a RUN of our program. The OUTPUT is a series of "pay forms" which can be cut out and inserted in the employee's pay envelope along with his check.

```
RUN


PROGRAM TO COMPUTE PAYROLL

AFTER ALL EMPLOYEES' DATA HAVE BEEN TYPED IN,
    TYPE A ZERO FOR THE EMPLOYEE NUMBER.  THEN
    THE PAYROLL WILL BE PRINTED OUT.

EMPLOYEE NUMBER =?123
HOURS WORKED =?39
PAY RATE =?3.78
SAVINGS PLAN =?15

EMPLOYEE NUMBER =?99
HOURS WORKED =?51
PAY RATE =?5.45
SAVINGS PLAN =?20

EMPLOYEE NUMBER =?0

===========================================================
===========================================================

EMPLOYEE NUMBER = 123

                              NORMAL PAY       = 147.42
                              OVERTIME         = 0
                              TOTAL GROSS PAY  = 147.42
DEDUCTIONS...
   SAVINGS PLAN: 15
   TAX WITHHELD: 22.113

                              TOTAL DEDUCTIONS = 37.113

                              NET PAY          = 110.31


===========================================================
===========================================================

EMPLOYEE NUMBER = 99

                              NORMAL PAY       = 218
                              OVERTIME         = 89.925
                              TOTAL GROSS PAY  = 307.925
DEDUCTIONS...
   SAVINGS PLAN: 20
   TAX WITHHELD: 61.585

                              TOTAL DEDUCTIONS = 81.585

                              NET PAY          = 226.34


===========================================================
```

Here is a LISTing of the /PAYROLL/ program:

```
10    PRINT "PROGRAM TO COMPUTE PAYROLL"
20    PRINT
30    PRINT "AFTER ALL EMPLOYEES' DATA HAVE BEEN TYPED IN,"
40    PRINT "   TYPE A ZERO FOR THE EMPLOYEE NUMBER.   THEN"
50    PRINT "   THE PAYROLL WILL BE PRINTED OUT."
60    PRINT
70    LET N=1
80    PRINT "EMPLOYEE NUMBER =";
90    INPUT E[N]
100   IF E[N]=0 THEN 200
110   PRINT "HOURS WORKED =";
120   INPUT H[N]
130   PRINT "PAY RATE =";
140   INPUT R[N]
150   PRINT "SAVINGS PLAN =";
160   INPUT S[N]
170   LET N=N+1
180   PRINT
190   GO TO 80
200   LET N=N-1
210   FOR I=1 TO N
220   PRINT
230   PRINT "================================================================"
240   PRINT "================================================================"
250   PRINT
260   PRINT "EMPLOYEE NUMBER =";E[I]
270   LET O1=0
280   IF H[I] <= 40 THEN 320
290   LET O1=(H[I]-40)*R[I]*1.5
300   LET G=40*R[I]
310   GO TO 330
320   LET G=H[I]*R[I]
330   PRINT TAB(29);"NORMAL PAY          =";G
340   PRINT TAB(29);"OVERTIME            =";O1
350   LET T=G+O1
360   PRINT TAB(29);"TOTAL GROSS PAY     =";T
370   PRINT "DEDUCTIONS..."
380   PRINT "  SAVINGS PLAN:";S[I]
390   IF T>50 THEN 420
400   LET F=0
410   GO TO 520
420   IF T>75 THEN 450
430   LET F=T*.05
440   GO TO 520
450   IF T>100 THEN 480
460   LET F=T*.1
470   GO TO 520
480   IF T>150 THEN 510
490   LET F=T*.15
500   GO TO 520
510   LET F=T*.2
520   PRINT "  TAX WITHHELD:";F
530   LET D=S[I]+F
540   PRINT TAB(29);"TOTAL DEDUCTIONS =";D
550   PRINT
560   PRINT TAB(29);"NET PAY             =";INT((T-D)*100+.5)/100
570   PRINT
580   NEXT I
590   PRINT
600   PRINT "================================================================"
610   END
```

Checks to see if employee worked "normal" or "overtime" hours.

Uses the "overtime" formula to calculate "time-and-a-half" pay.

Lines 300 and 320 use the "normal" formula to calculate normal pay.

Calculates "gross" pay.

Lines 390 to 510 are used to find out in which "tax bracket" the gross pay falls and then to calculate the amount of tax to be withheld.

Suggested Explorations:

1. Write a program that keeps track of your checking account. It should add in deposits, subtract the amounts of checks you write, subtract the monthly and/or individual check charge the bank makes, and print the balance for any date.

2. Write a program that prints out monthly bills for a credit-card company. It should add in payments made in the past month, subtract the cost of purchases made, and subtract a 1.5% monthly finance charge on the unpaid balance. (NOTE: A monthly 1.5% finance charge=18% yearly charge.)

3. It is often desirable to put records in order, either alphabetically or numerically. Below is a subroutine that can be added to the /PAYROLL/ program that will *sort* the pay records by employee number. You'll have to add a new line

205 GOSUB 1000

to PAYROLL, and change

610 END to 610 STOP.

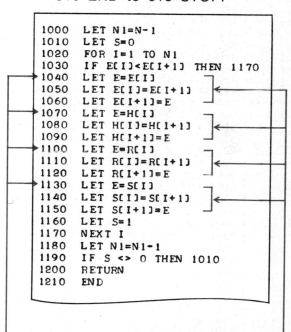

```
1000   LET N1=N-1
1010   LET S=0
1020   FOR I=1 TO N1
1030   IF E[I]<E[I+1] THEN 1170
1040   LET E=E[I]
1050   LET E[I]=E[I+1]
1060   LET E[I+1]=E
1070   LET E=H[I]
1080   LET H[I]=H[I+1]
1090   LET H[I+1]=E
1100   LET E=R[I]
1110   LET R[I]=R[I+1]
1120   LET R[I+1]=E
1130   LET E=S[I]
1140   LET S[I]=S[I+1]
1150   LET S[I+1]=E
1160   LET S=1
1170   NEXT I
1180   LET N1=N1-1
1190   IF S <> 0 THEN 1010
1200   RETURN
1210   END
```

E is a temporary variable used in swapping.
(Recall the //SORT// program in Section 3–2.)

The list E(I) is sorted in increasing order, and the lists H(I), R(I), and S(I) are rearranged to match.

4. Can you change your program so that it sorts the pay records in order of increasing net pay?

4–5 Batch-Mode Computing

Computing done at a terminal connected to a computer that "speaks" BASIC is often called "interactive," since there is give-and-take between the machine and the programmer.

For many applications, however, interactive computing is not needed. For example, the job of preparing payroll checks does not require that a human being be in constant communication with the computer, watching each piece of information it prints. It suffices that the instructions for preparing these checks be programmed just once, and that the computer then be left by itself to grind out the checks, with the human operator picking them up later in the day. The diagram below illustrates a typical batch system.

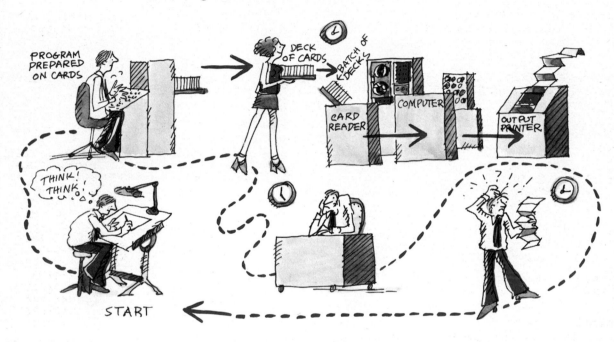

After designing his program at his desk, the user "writes" his program on cards. This is done either by making special pencil marks on the card or by punching holes in the card. He then takes his "deck" of cards to the computer room and places it on a stack (batch) of decks from other users. The card reader interprets the statements on the cards by decoding the marks on them. The computer then executes the programs that were on the cards, and prints the output. The programmer may have to wait a few hours since batch systems are often used for very long-running programs. If there are mistakes, or if revisions must be made, the whole process must be repeated. Just one warning: if you are using a batch computer, you can't use INPUT statements (why?). Use READ-DATA instead.

Selected Answers and Hints for Exercises

Section 2-2, page 23
Exercise 2(f): $(4+(9*2))*(3+1)=88$

Section 2-3, page 34
Exercise 1: The variables C23, XY, 2D, 5F, W13, IOU, F-2, 3, and X3.1 are not allowed in BASIC.
Exercise 2: The program output is:
12 8 20 4 96
248

Section 2-4, page 45
Exercise 9: (a) 314159000000
            (b) .0000000000314159
Exercise 10: (a) 7.00000E+09
             (b) 7.00000E−09

Section 2-5, page 49
Exercise 2: For R=2, the RUN looks like this:

```
PROGRAM TO FIND AREA OF A CIRCLE

TYPE IN RADIUS
?2
AREA = 12.5664
```

Exercise 3: For example, in line 60, the right quotation mark is missing; in line 80, the quotation marks should not be used.

Section 2-6, page 57
Exercise 2, #8: TRUE, 16*48 is less than 24*48; branch to line 80.

Section 2-7, page 70
Exercise 1: For example, the variable M8 takes on the values in the set {3,9,15,21,27}.
Exercise 2: For example, the variable X is made to take on the given set of values by the statement:
FOR X=1 TO 1.7 STEP .1
Exercise 4: Ten numbers will be printed in all.

Pages 73-74
Exercise 2: The pattern will be:

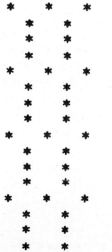

Exercise 3: Three lines, with six asterisks on each line.

/BLOCKS/ - Use 3 nested FOR loops: The outer loop will control the number of rectangles (3), the middle loop will control the number of rows per rectangle (4), and the inner loop will control the number of asterisks per row (7).

```
10  FOR I=1 TO 3
20  FOR J=1 TO 4
30  FOR K=1 TO 7
40  PRINT "*";
50  NEXT K
60  PRINT
70  NEXT J
80  PRINT
90  NEXT I
100 END
```

Page 76
///SPEED CAR///

STARTING SPEED (MILES/HOUR)	FINAL SPEED (AFTER 10TH TRIP AROUND)
.5	22.6296
1	45.2593
1.5	67.8889
2	90.5185
2.5	113.148
3	135.778
3.5	158.407
4	181.037
4.5	203.667
5	226.296
5.5	248.926
6	271.556

Section 3-2, pages 88-90
Exercise 1: For example, Z(16), Z(160/10), Z(256/16)
Exercise 2: 18
           16
           10
           130
            .
            .
            .
Exercise 3: ?12
           ?13
           ?14
           ?15
           ?16

YOUR NUMBERS	SQ. OF YOUR NO.
12	144
13	169
14	196
15	225
16	256

Section 3-2 (continued)

Modification of /TRACK1/:
Add the following steps:

```
291    PRINT
292    PRINT "INPUT ATHLETE NUMBERS FOR 3 BEST SPEEDS;"
293    INPUT A,B,C
294    LET S1=(300/5280)/(T[A]/3600)
295    LET S2=(300/5280)/(T[B]/3600)
296    LET S3=(300/5280)/(T[C]/3600)
297    PRINT "AVERAGE SPEED OF TOP 3 WAS";
298    PRINT (S1+S2+S3)/3;" MPH."
```

Section 3-4, page 100
A program for //BRAKE//

```
10     PRINT "DISTANCE NEEDED TO STOP A CAR AT VARIOUS SPEEDS"
20     PRINT
30     PRINT "SPEED          DISTANCE (EACH + REPRESENTS ONE CAR LENGTH)"
40     LET D=0
50     PRINT TAB(4);
60     FOR N=1 TO 66
70     PRINT "+";
80     NEXT N
90     PRINT
100    PRINT
110    IF D>0 THEN 180
120    FOR I=10 TO 80 STEP 5
130    LET D=I*I*.01
140    PRINT I; TAB(D+3);"*"
150    NEXT I
160    PRINT
170    GOTO 50
180    END
```

Section 3-5, page 105
Exercise 4: Output is: 2
                     1

Section 3-6, pages 111-112
Modification of /PIZZA/:
Find the cost per bite by dividing the cost (for example, $1.00 for a 10″ pizza) by the number of square-inch bites (78.5397 for a 10″ pizza). The best buy will be the pizza with the lowest cost per bite (this is the same idea as unit pricing in supermarkets).

HINT for //INVERSE PIZZA//:
If P = no. of people, B = no. of bites each, and N = no. of pizzas:

$$LET\ D = 2 * SQR(P * B/(3.14159*N))$$

Pages 118-119
Exercise 5: Change line 20 in /RAND/ to:
        20 PRINT INT(101*RND(1)−50)

Hint for /DICE/:
Use a variable for the toss of each die.
For example:

        LET A = INT(6*RND(1)+1)
        LET B = INT(6*RND(1)+1)
        PRINT A, B, A+B

Hint for //GUESS//:
To find which player was closer to the computer's choice, you might do the following:
    Use P1 as player one's number, P2 as player two's number, C as the computer's choice, and then use a conditional statement of the form:
        IF ABS(C−P1)<ABS(C−P2) THEN . . .
(We use ABS to get the numerical "distance" from C to P1 and P2.)
    If the condition is true, P1 wins. If the condition is not true and the players gave different numbers, then P2 wins.
    What do you want the computer to do if the second player uses the same number as the first player?

Section 3–6 (continued)

Pages 122–123
Comments on /MELODY/:

DO, RE, MI, FA, SOL, LA, TI stand for different notes of a scale: DO is the first, RE is the next (one tone higher), and so on. Listen to the song "DO RE MI" from *The Sound of Music* to get an idea of what these notes sound like.

Hints for //SONG//: End each song with DO.
(1) For a simple program, you might select several bars as in /MELODY/:

DO MI SOL, LA FA RE, and so on

You can then have the computer randomly select 4 of these to make each line except the last. Make special provisions to end with DO.
(2) For a more complicated program, you can have the computer make up each bar by making 3 or 4 random selections from the 7 possible notes.
(3) You can extend the possibilities by using DO1 as the upper octave of DO.
(4) Here's an example with four bars per line.

```
5    RANDOMIZE       (SEE PAGE 116.)
10   FOR L=1 TO 4
20   FOR B=1 TO 3
30   GOTO INT(3*RND(1)+1) OF 40,60,80
40   PRINT ": LA TI   ";
50   GOTO 90
60   PRINT ": SOL MI ";
70   GOTO 90
80   PRINT ": FA RE   ";
90   NEXT B
100  IF L<4 THEN 120
110  GOTO 170
120  GOTO INT(2*RND(1)+1) OF 130,150
130  PRINT ": SOL - :"
140  GOTO 160
150  PRINT ": MI - :"
160  NEXT L
170  PRINT ": DO - :"
180  END
RUN


: FA RE  : LA TI  : LA TI  : MI -   :
: FA RE  : SOL MI : SOL MI : SOL -  :
: LA TI  : SOL MI : FA RE  : SOL -  :
: SOL MI : LA TI  : SOL MI : DO -   :
```

Section 4-3, page 140

Quizzes make interesting game programs, especially when the RND function is used.

Here are two examples that may give you some ideas.

```
5   RANDOMIZE        (SEE PAGE 116.)
10  LET W=0
20  LET R=0
30  PRINT "QUIZ ON  SPEED = DISTANCE/TIME"
40  PRINT
50  FOR I=1 TO 5
60  LET D=INT((3*RND(1)+1)*100)
70  LET T=(INT(5*RND(1)+5))/10
80  PRINT "AIRPLANE";I;" GOES";D;" MILES IN";T;" HOURS."
90  PRINT "WHAT IS ITS SPEED IN MPH";
100  INPUT S1
110  LET S=D/T
120  IF ABS(INT(S1-S)) <= 2 THEN 160
130  PRINT "NO: SPEED = D/T =";D;"/";T;" =";S;" MPH"
140  LET W=W+1
150  GOTO 180
160  PRINT "VERY GOOD!  THE EXACT ANSWER IS";S;" MPH."
170  LET R=R+1
180  PRINT
190  NEXT I
200  PRINT
210  PRINT "SCORE:  ";R;" RIGHT, ";W;" WRONG"
220  LET P=R/5*100
230  PRINT "PERCENTAGE RIGHT:";P;"%"
240  END
RUN


QUIZ ON  SPEED = DISTANCE/TIME

AIRPLANE 1 GOES 107 MILES IN .8 HOURS.
WHAT IS ITS SPEED IN MPH?134
VERY GOOD!  THE EXACT ANSWER IS 133.75 MPH.

AIRPLANE 2 GOES 311 MILES IN .6 HOURS.
WHAT IS ITS SPEED IN MPH?520
VERY GOOD!  THE EXACT ANSWER IS 518.333 MPH.

AIRPLANE 3 GOES 127 MILES IN .6 HOURS.
WHAT IS ITS SPEED IN MPH?212
VERY GOOD!  THE EXACT ANSWER IS 211.667 MPH.

AIRPLANE 4 GOES 399 MILES IN .9 HOURS.
WHAT IS ITS SPEED IN MPH?440
NO: SPEED = D/T = 399/ .9 = 443.333 MPH

AIRPLANE 5 GOES 251 MILES IN .5 HOURS.
WHAT IS ITS SPEED IN MPH?502
VERY GOOD!  THE EXACT ANSWER IS 502 MPH.


SCORE:  4 RIGHT,  1 WRONG
PERCENTAGE RIGHT: 80%
```

152

```
5    RANDOMIZE     (SEE PAGE 116.)
10   PRINT "THIS IS AN 'IQ'-TYPE QUIZ."
20   PRINT
30   PRINT "THIS PROGRAM WILL PRINT VARIOUS SEQUENCES OF NUMBERS"
40   PRINT "EACH ENDING WITH A BLANK (-----).   WHEN YOU SEE A '?',"
50   PRINT "TYPE IN THE NUMBER THAT YOU THINK THE COMPUTER MIGHT"
60   PRINT "HAVE PRINTED IN PLACE OF THE BLANK."
70   PRINT
80   LET R=0
90   LET W=0
100   FOR I=1 TO 5
110   PRINT "PROBLEM"; I
120   LET A=INT(10*RND(1)+1)
130   LET B=INT(10*RND(1)+1)
140   LET G=INT(3*RND(1)+1)
150   IF A>B THEN 290
160   GO TO G OF 170,210,250
170   LET X=2*A+3*B
180   PRINT A;",";B;",";A+B;",";A+2*B;", -----"
190   INPUT Y
200   GO TO 410
210   LET X=A*A*B*B*B.
220   PRINT A;",";B;",";A*B;",";B*A*B;", -----"
230   INPUT Y
240   GO TO 410
250   LET X=-B
260   PRINT A;",";B;",";B-A;",";-A;", -----"
270   INPUT Y
280   GO TO 410
290   GO TO G OF 300,400,380
300   LET X=A*5
310   PRINT A;",";2*A;",";3*A;",";4*A;", -----"
320   INPUT Y
330   GO TO 410
340   LET X=16*A
350   PRINT A;",";2*A;",";4*A;",";8*A;", -----"
360   INPUT Y
370   GO TO 410
380   LET X=A↑5
390   PRINT A;",";A*A;",";A↑3;",";A↑4;", -----"
400   INPUT Y
410   IF X=Y THEN 450
420   PRINT "NO; THE COMPUTER'S SEQUENCE HAS";X;"."
430   LET W=W+1
440   GO TO 470
450   PRINT "THAT'S RIGHT!"
460   LET R=R+1
470   PRINT
480   NEXT I
490   PRINT
500   PRINT "SCORE:    ";R;" RIGHT, ";W;" WRONG"
510   END
RUN


THIS IS AN 'IQ'-TYPE QUIZ.

THIS PROGRAM WILL PRINT VARIOUS SEQUENCES OF NUMBERS
EACH ENDING WITH A BLANK (-----).   WHEN YOU SEE A '?',
TYPE IN THE NUMBER THAT YOU THINK THE COMPUTER MIGHT
HAVE PRINTED IN PLACE OF THE BLANK.

PROBLEM 1
 8, 16, 24, 32, -----
?40
THAT'S RIGHT!
```

```
PROBLEM 5
 7, 8, 56, 448, -----
?25088
THAT'S RIGHT!


SCORE:    4 RIGHT,  1 WRONG
```

Index

Summary of BASIC

STATEMENTS (require line numbers)

Name and page	Purpose	Example
PRINT (page 19)	Types out messages ⟶ or values of numerical expressions ⟶ or both ⟶	170 PRINT "HELLO THERE" 200 PRINT X, 3*X+5, 4↑6 220 PRINT "ANSWERS="; X+9; 4↑6; Y
LET (page 29)	Calculates an expression and assigns the value to a given location.	50 LET Y=7 60 LET X=2*B+X
INPUT (page 37)	Requests data for certain variables from the terminal (during a RUN). ⟶	380 INPUT A,B
GOTO (page 46)	Sends the program execution to another line. ⟶	60 GOTO 205
IF . . . THEN (page 52)	Sends the program execution to the given line if the condition is true. ⟶	90 IF W8<=4 THEN 260
FOR (STEP) (pages 63, 68)	Sets up and runs the body of a loop a stated number of times. ⟶	40 FOR I=1 TO 9 STEP 2 ⬚ Body of the loop
NEXT (page 63)	Closes the loop. ⟶	80 NEXT I
DIM (pages 87, 96)	Declares maximum sizes of arrays. ⟶	150 DIM M(20),N(15,20)
REM (page 89)	Permits comments. ⟶	105 REM CALCULATES AREA
TAB (page 97)	Permits computed placement of output. ⟶	160 PRINT TAB(X); "*"
READ (page 100)	Assigns values from DATA statements to given variables. ⟶	150 READ A(J),B(J),C
DATA (page 100)	Holds the data (values) for READ statements. ⟶	200 DATA 2,3,6
RESTORE (page 104)	Allows data to be used again. ⟶	238 RESTORE
GOTO . . . OF (page 120) (ON . . . GOTO, page 121)	Sends the program execution to one of several lines depending on the value of the variable.	310 GOTO Y OF 35,90,125 (310 ON Y GOTO 35,90,125)
GOSUB (page 123)	Sends the program execution to a subroutine. ⟶	40 GOSUB 300 50 ------ ← 60 ------ 300 ----- 310 -----
RETURN (page 123)	Sends the program execution back to the line after GOSUB. ⟶	320 RETURN
RANDOMIZE (page 116)	"Randomizes" the random number generator (only on some computers). ⟶	5 RANDOMIZE
STOP (page 56)	Halts RUN of program (may be anywhere within the program). ⟶	65 STOP
END (page 19)	Last line of program.	999 END

COMMANDS (need no line numbers)

LIST (page 13)	Prints out the current program.	Other commands vary from computer to computer. Check your reference manual.
RUN (page 14)	Begins execution of the program.	
SCR (page 26)	Erases the current program.	

MISCELLANEOUS

Variables: X,Y3,C(Y),N(X,Y),F(B(X),J) Operators: +,−,*,/,↑ (page 21) Relations: <,<=,=,>,>=,<> (pages 54, 56)
(pages 30, 34, 85, 94)
Functions: SQR, INT, ABS, RND (pages 109–119) [Also available: SIN, COS, TAN, ATN, LOG, EXP, SGN]